Leadership Lessons from Silicon Valley

How to Survive and Thrive in Disruptive Times

Rebecca L. Morgan, CSP, CMC

Leadership Lessons from Silicon Valley: How to Survive and Thrive in Disruptive Times

Printed in the United States of America.

ISBN eBook: 978-1-930039-44-5

Printed book: 978-1-930039-43-8

How to order:

Quantity copies may be ordered directly from www.RebeccaMorgan.com.

Go to RebeccaMorgan.com/SV for links to reports, assessments, and other resources.

How to Use This Book

This book is for anyone interested in becoming a better leader. It's full of reports from my reading on the subject, my personal experiences, observations, and lessons. There are exercises throughout where you are asked to write down how you'll apply the information. You'll get more out of this if you take a few minutes to write down your thoughts in those areas.

How to use this book

☆ *Determine how you can use ideas:* A concept put into action has much more value than just knowing the idea.

☆ *Learn from "OPE" — Other People's Experiences:* If you're astute, you learn from your own life experiences. Some of these are positive — some are negative. It is less painful to learn from other people's unpleasant experiences!

☆ *Share with your teammates:* Order a copy for everyone on your team. Assign a chapter to read before a staff meeting. Then discuss the ideas at that meeting. Facilitate a discussion to adapt the lessons to help each person become more effective.

Books by
Rebecca L. Morgan

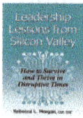

Leadership Lessons from Silicon Valley: How to Survive and Thrive in Disruptive Times

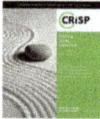

Calming Upset Customers: Stay in Control ... in Any Situation

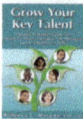

Grow Your Key Talent: Thought-Provoking Essays for Business Owners, Executives and Managers on Developing Star Staff

Life's Lessons: Insights and Information for a Richer Life

Professional Selling: Practical Secrets for Successful Sales

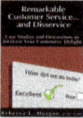

Remarkable Customer Service ... and Disservice: Case Studies and Discussions to Increase Your Customers' Delight

All can be ordered at www.RebeccaMorgan.com

About the Author

Rebecca L. Morgan is an internationally recognized consultant, trainer, facilitator, and speaker, based in San José, CA.

Rebecca partners with clients to create innovative, long-lasting professional development solutions. Her focus is on leadership development implementation, strategic customer service, and increasing workplace effectiveness by providing the right skills for the right people in the right way.

Many recognizable organizations have engaged Rebecca to develop creative solutions to their situations. These include: Apple, Singapore Airlines, Wells Fargo Bank, New York Life Insurance, Microsoft, ING, Hewlett-Packard, Adobe, Applied Materials, Quantum, Seagate, Lockheed Martin, Sony, AIG, and Stanford University, among many more.

Rebecca is a respected professional development consultant, bestselling author, and speaker.

Her media appearances include 60 Minutes, The Oprah Winfrey Show, National Public Radio's Market Place, *USA Today*, *Wall Street Journal*, Forbes.com, *San José Mercury News*, Malaysia's *Star* newspaper, Singapore's *Straight Times, the Brunei Times, The Asian Journal*, and the *San Francisco Chronicle*. Her ideas are so solid that Microsoft hired her as its workplace effectiveness spokesperson.

Rebecca's books, recordings, videos, and learning tools exemplify the excellence she creates in all of her work. She's authored 27 popular books — two of which have been translated into nine languages.

One of an Elite Few Professionals

Rebecca is committed to continuous learning and growing, especially since that is what she imparts to others. She has demonstrated this striving by receiving the Certified Speaking Professional (CSP) designation conferred by the National Speakers Association (NSA). At the time, the ten-year-old designation had been earned by only 215 people in the world—less than seven percent of the 3700 members of NSA.

She has also earned the professional designation Certified Management Consultant (CMC) from the Institute of Management Consultants (IMC). She is the fifteenth professional in the world to earn both the CSP and the CMC designations.

More information on Rebecca's services is at www. RebeccaMorgan.com

Contents

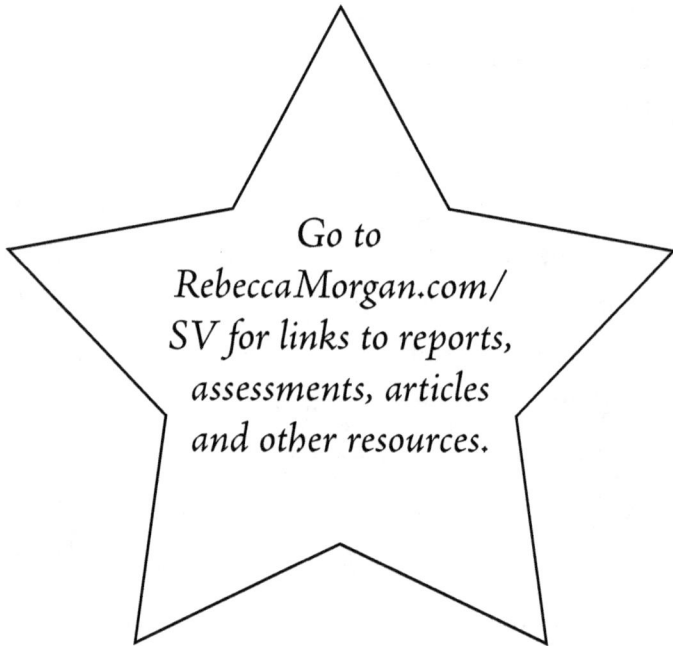

Go to RebeccaMorgan.com/ SV for links to reports, assessments, articles and other resources.

Leading in Disruptive Times

John Chambers
Former Exec. Chairman & CEO CISCO

"Disrupt, or get disrupted."

© 2019, www.RebeccaMorgan.com

Photo: © Remy Steinegger/steineggerpix.com

John Chambers had it right. If you are not disrupting your industry, you will soon be disrupted by someone who is.

We'll explore how you can survive and thrive during disruptive times using examples from Silicon Valley companies and even some which aren't.

How has disruption affected you positively or negatively?

_____

_____

_____

_____

_____

The term "disruption" can be confusing. Let's examine what disruption is and isn't.

What are some of the key elements of disruption?

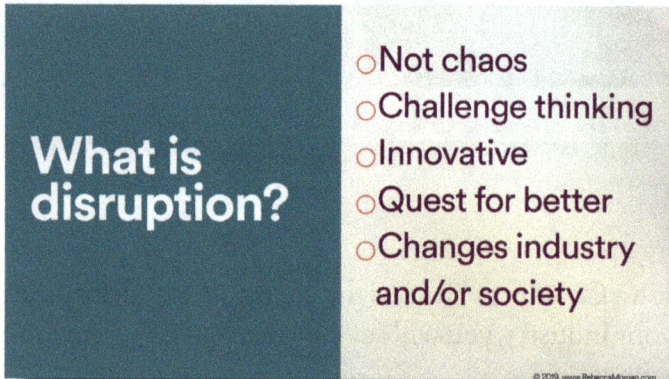

_____

_____

_____

What is disruption?	○ Not chaos ○ Challenge thinking ○ Innovative ○ Quest for better ○ Changes industry and/or society

© 2019, www.RebeccaMorgan.com

It's not necessarily chaos

Although disruption does not necessarily cause chaos, and chaos does not mean something is disruptive, any change — positive or negative — creates stress for many people. It can feel chaotic.

One of Facebook's founding values, "Move fast and break things," shows it prepares employees to break things that are working in a quest to make them better.

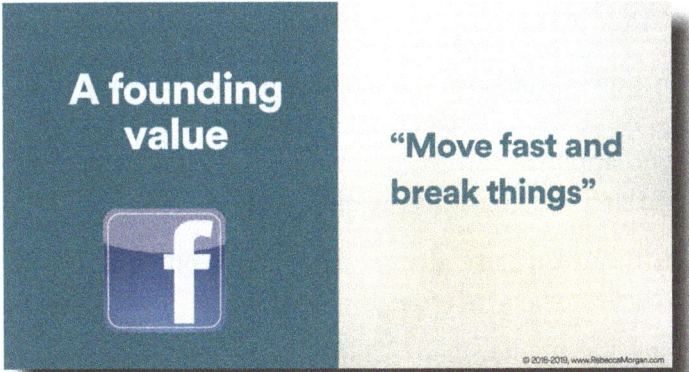

Can you think of something you've purposefully "broken" to make it better? Note it here.

_____

_____

_____

Challenge thinking

True disruption challenges our way of thinking. You have to discontinue thinking the status quo is the right way. In fact, contrarian thinking helps you reexamine how you've always done something to see if there's a more effective way to do it.

When has your thinking been challenged and it created a better outcome?

_____

_____

_____

Innovative

Innovation comes when a new way of thinking is applied to a challenge. This sometimes happens when you apply an idea from another industry or application to your current problem.

Innovation isn't always disruptive, but disruption nearly always includes innovation.

You have to begin by seeking to disrupt yourself first by challenging your own thinking. Bill Taylor said it well in his *Harvard Business Review* article on Netflix:

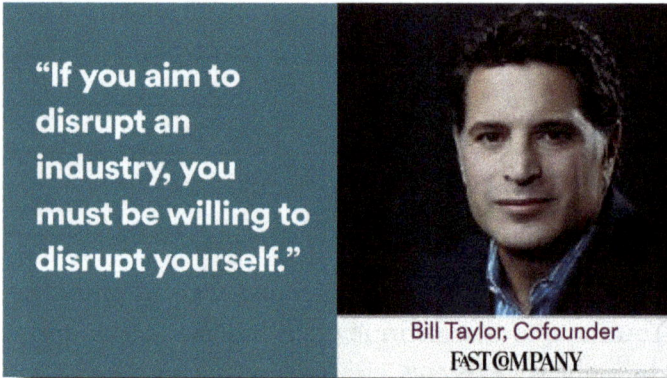

"If you aim to disrupt an industry, you must be willing to disrupt yourself."

Bill Taylor, Cofounder
FAST COMPANY

How could you purposefully disrupt your own thinking? Which contrarians could you consult? Which media could you read/watch that is 180 degrees from your current thinking?

_____

_____

_____

Quest for better

Disruption can happen when someone is dissatisfied with the current solution and seeks for a better one.

Steve Jobs famously created new products that he wanted to use, knowing customers would often follow his lead. He came up with the idea of the iPod because he wanted to carry 1000 songs in his pocket The technology of the day — the portable CD player — could only hold one CD.

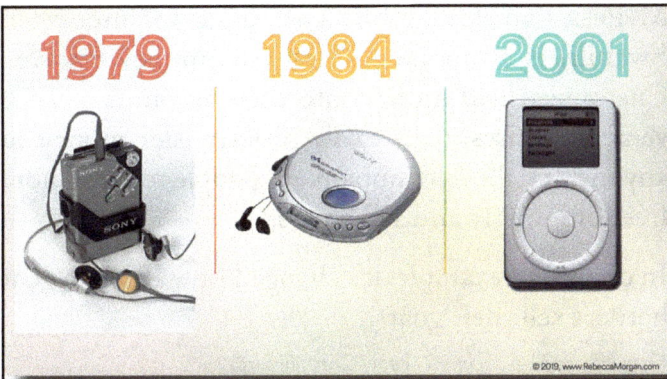

Changes industry and/or society

The most common use of the word "disruption" nowadays denotes a company or product that significantly changes an industry or society.

Which companies or products come to mind that fit this description?

_____

_____

M-Pesa ("m" for mobile and "pesa" for money in Swahili) is a mobile phone-based money transfer. Customers load money into their accounts at convenience stores, then easily text transfer money to anyone. It's allowed "unbanked" people to have more freedom to buy and sell goods.

In one small example, it's changed how Kenyan goat herders sell their goats.

More info on M-pesa: http://bit.ly/GoatBillboard/.

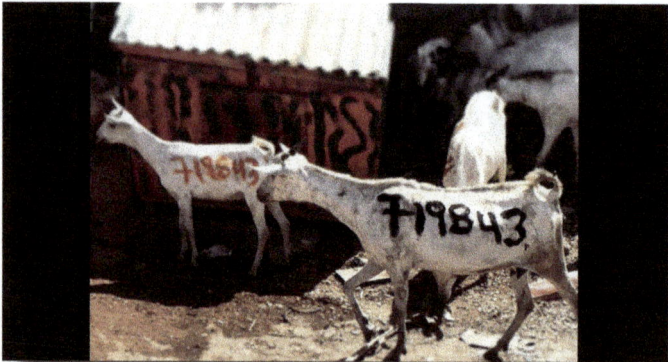

Disruption from Technology

We've seen many manufacturing jobs replaced by robots. We're beginning to see disruption because of automation in industries previously thought to be immune. The predicted numbers are staggering for how artificial intelligence will change work for millions.

We're seeing innovators in transportation, security, and other industries thought to require humans.

What examples of disruption from technology have you witnessed?

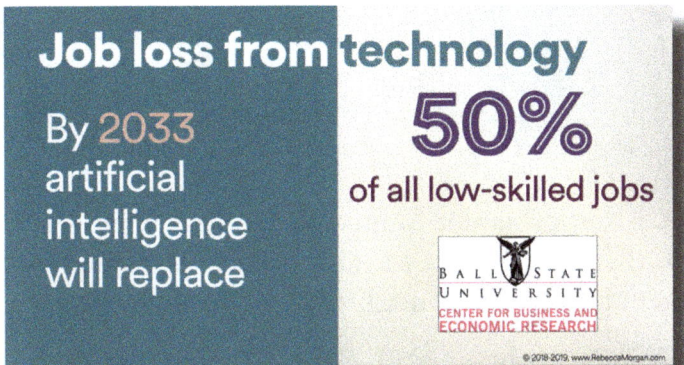

_____

_____

_____

Job loss from technology

By 2033 artificial intelligence will replace

50% of all low-skilled jobs

BALL STATE UNIVERSITY
CENTER FOR BUSINESS AND ECONOMIC RESEARCH

© 2018-2019, www.RebeccaMorgan.com

Source: Ball State University's Center for Business and Economic Research, "How Vulnerable Are American Communities to Automation, Trade and Urbanization?", 2017.

Job loss from technology

By 2033 artificial intelligence will replace

38% of *all* US jobs.

pwc

© 2018-2019, www.RebeccaMorgan.com

Source: PricewaterhouseCoopers 2017 study, "Will Robots Steal Our Jobs?"

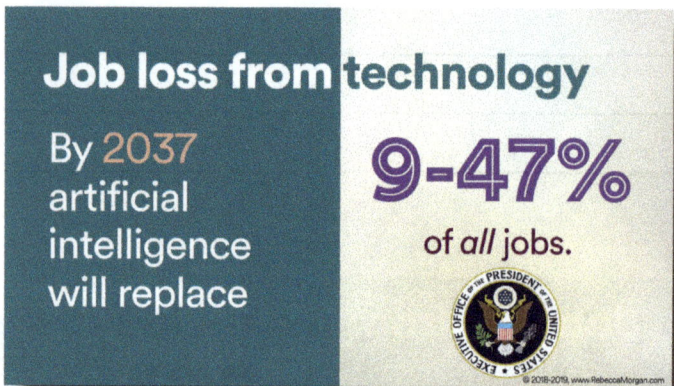

Job loss from technology

By 2037 artificial intelligence will replace

9-47% of *all* jobs.

© 2018-2019, www.RebeccaMorgan.com

Source: President Obama's White House study, Dec. 2016

Disruption is not limited to artificial intelligence. Other technologies will also impact companies' current processes and markets.

A joint study by *MIT Sloan Management Review* and Deloitte points to other disruptive trends. The question is not if your company will be disrupted, but how you can prepare for the coming disruption.

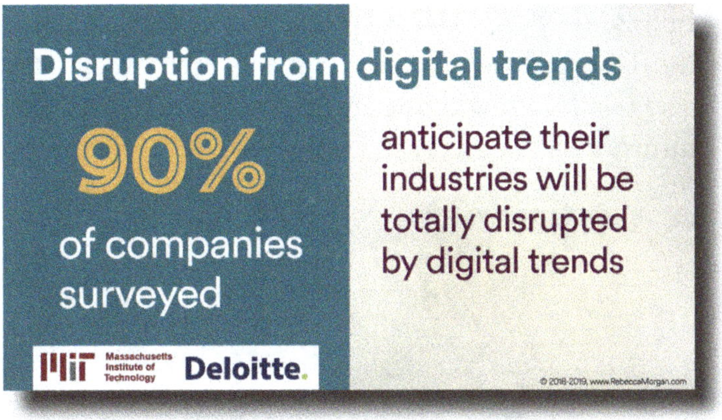

Disruption from digital trends

90%
of companies surveyed

anticipate their industries will be totally disrupted by digital trends

Massachusetts Institute of Technology | Deloitte.

© 2018-2019, www.RebeccaMorgan.com

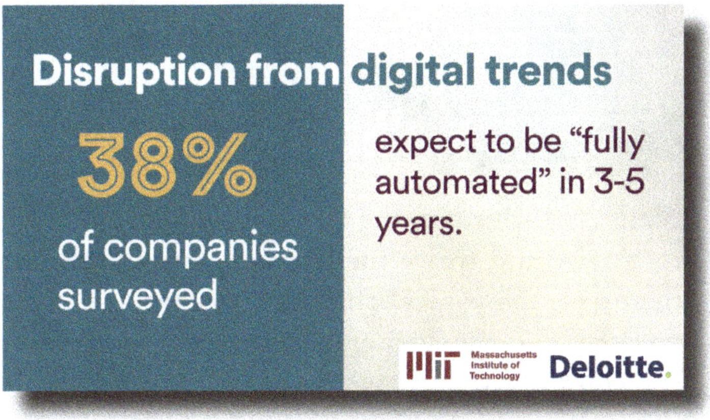

Disruption from digital trends

38%
of companies surveyed

expect to be "fully automated" in 3-5 years.

Massachusetts Institute of Technology | Deloitte.

Think about how these numbers will affect your life and those you care about. What could be the ramifications?

_____

_____

_____

In July, 2018, KPMG released "Five Forces Shaping the Tech Industry," a survey of 104 tech executives. The results show that they are optimistic about the future.

KPMG

98% See technological disruption as more of an opportunity than a threat.

© 2018, www.RebeccaMorgan.com

Nearly two-thirds of the CEOs realize that in order to survive and thrive they have to actively disrupt their own companies. They have to continue to innovate, encourage every employee to think differently, and continually challenge the status quo.

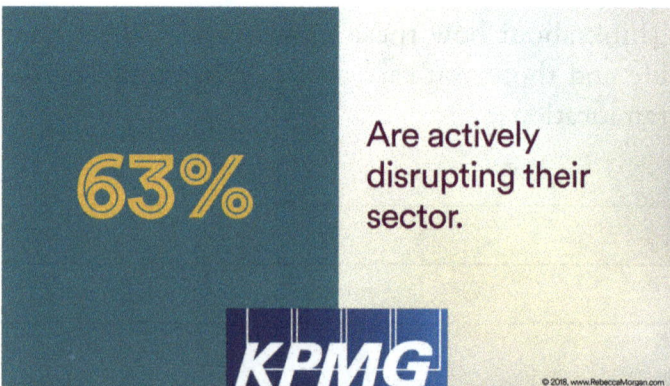

63% Are actively disrupting their sector.

KPMG

© 2018, www.RebeccaMorgan.com

Continuing their optimism, sixty percent of the tech CEOs think technology will increase jobs, not decrease the total number. Of course, there will losses in some jobs, but overall they believe there will be a gain.

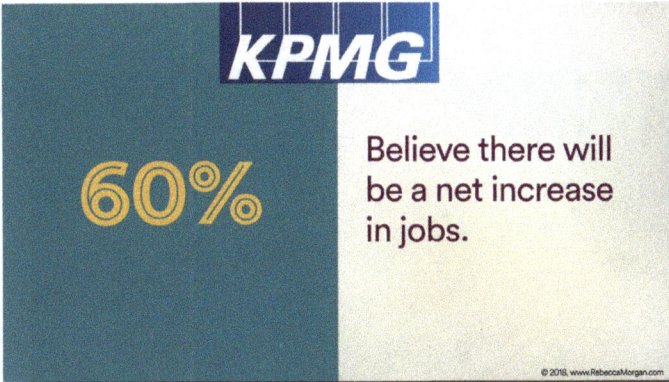

KPMG

60%

Believe there will be a net increase in jobs.

© 2018, www.RebeccaMorgan.com

The CEOs also point back to artificial intelligence and the pace at which it is creating disruption. You need to embrace disruption and disrupt your own organization proactively before competitors do so and you are reacting instead.

KPMG

"AI innovations are advancing at a staggering pace and will disrupt almost every business and industry."

© 2018, www.RebeccaMorgan.com

What can you do now to reskill your best employees whose jobs may be eliminated due to technology? It makes sense to start retraining great workers, rather than losing them when their jobs are eliminated. Think of all the time and money it takes to hire someone.

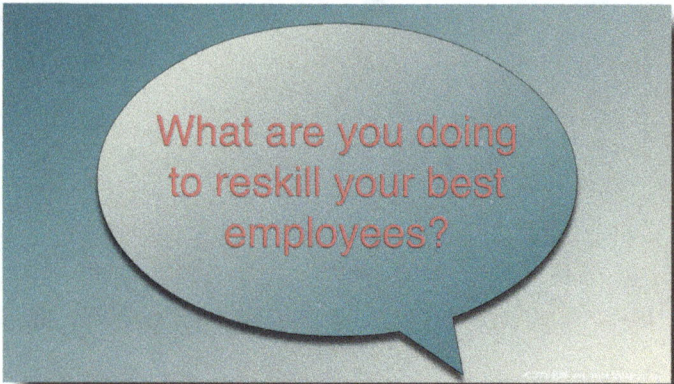

What are you doing now to ensure your best employees have a job with you? What more could you do to reskill them to prepare them for the jobs you'll need soon?

_____

_____

_____

_____

_____

People Replaced by Technology

Here are just a few examples of how AI is displacing humans. There are lots of other non-manufacturing examples, including using robots in food service, health care, retail, and many more industries.

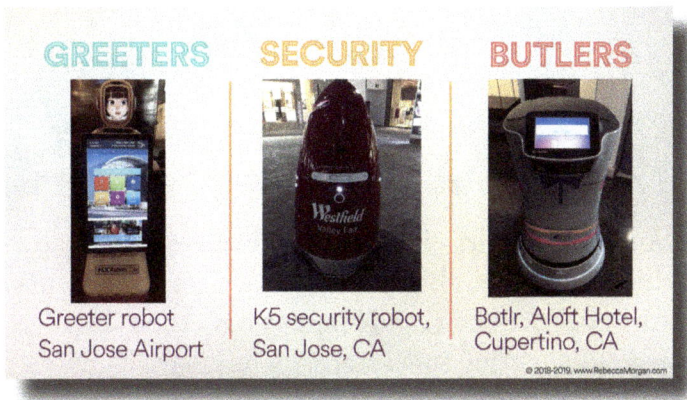

GREETERS — Greeter robot, San Jose Airport

SECURITY — K5 security robot, San Jose, CA

BUTLERS — Botlr, Aloft Hotel, Cupertino, CA

© 2018-2019. www.RebeccaMorgan.com

Robots are replacing some human labor in Silicon Valley.

- ☆ "Amelia" at San José Mineta International Airport interacts with passengers.

- ☆ Security robots roam the hallways and parking lots of a shopping mall, heading off hijinks.

- ☆ "Botlr" will deliver towels and even food to your door, calling you when he's arrived.

Environments Help with Disruption

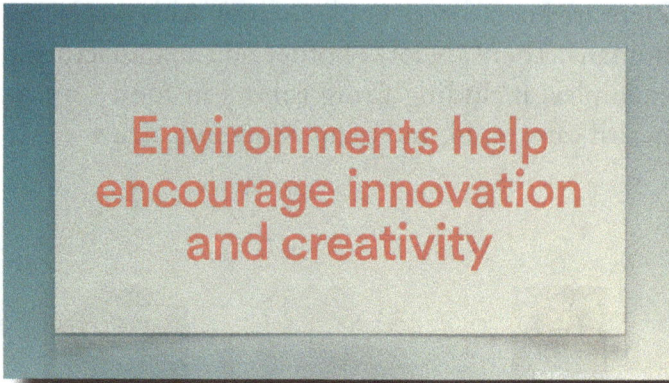

Environments help
encourage innovation
and creativity

Some companies encourage innovative and creative thinking through unusual office environments. Airbnb, Pixar, Box, and Zappos have their own way of implementing this idea.

Of course, the physical environment is only one way to prod innovative thinking.

How can you encourage more creativity in your environment without it being distracting?

_____

_____

_____

_____

Get your team's ideas on what to try. Have fun and experiment — you can always go back to the old way.

How do leaders create an environment for team members to seek change?

Airbnb's San Francisco headquarters has meeting spaces designed after the homes listed on their site. This is a break room duplicated in detail from a kitchen in a home in Italy listed on Airbnb.com

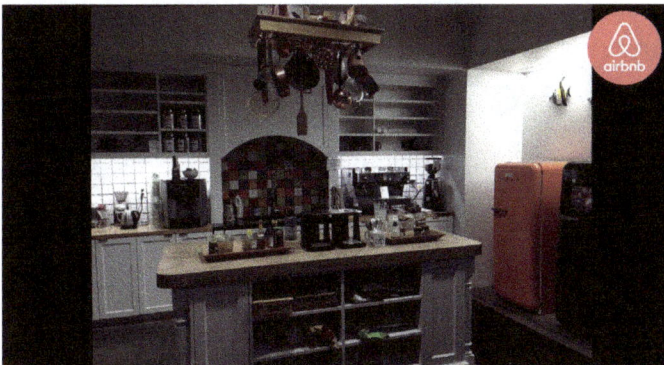

It may seem obvious, but people creating disruption have to seek change. However, change is stressful for some and therefore, makes it difficult to think creatively. It's hard to foster an environment that embraces change, but it's critical.

Disruption depends on *seeking* change.

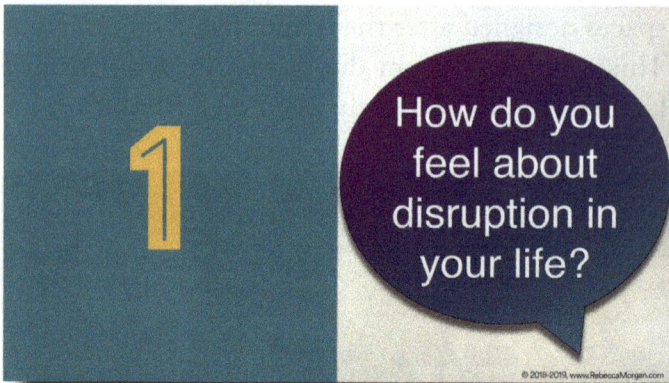

1

How do you feel about disruption in your life?

Write your answer here:

_____

_____

_____

_____

_____

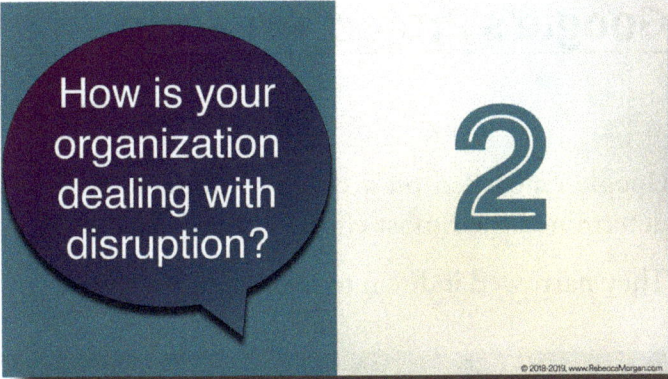

Write your answer here:

_____

_____

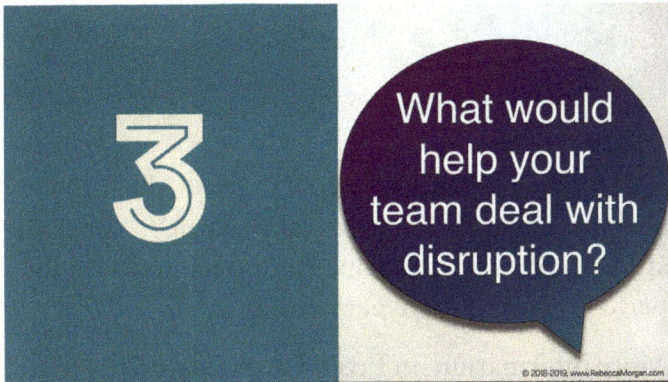

Write your answer here:

_____

_____

Google's Project Aristotle

Google embarked on a quest to understand what determined their most effective teams.

They narrowed it down to five elements.

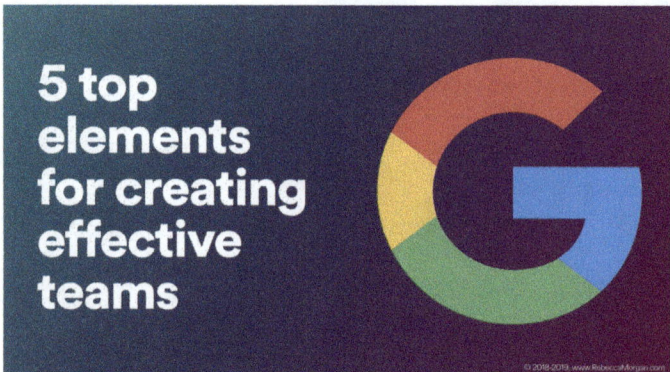

Headed by People Analytics Director Abeer Dubey, and Manager Julia Rozovsky, Project Aristotle studied a mix of departments and teams, both low-performing and high-performing.

More information on Project Aristotle can be found on rework.withgoogle.com, including discussion of the project, and worksheets for your use with your team.

The New York Times published an article on this as well, bit.ly/NYTAristotle/.

The comprehensive study included 180 Google teams worldwide. They ensured the best data by including both high and low-performing teams to see what was different about the high-performing ones.

The Project Aristotle team interviewed over 1500 Googlers. They identified and analyzed over 250 team attributes to whittle it down to the top five.

Photo: Hamilton83

Jack Welch said it well. You need a great team to bring ideas to fruition. That's why focusing on good team dynamics is so important. If a leader ignores what motivates their team members, they do so at their peril. That's why the Google research is so important.

The researchers explored what they considered to matter. However, they found that the important ones were those that seemingly did not matter.

List what you think *would not* matter on the most effective teams.

_____

_____

_____

_____

_____

_____

_____

_____

_____

_____

What doesn't matter?

- Teammates co-location
- Consensus-driven decision making
- Team members' extroversion
- Team members' individual performance
- Workload quantity
- Seniority
- Team size*

© 2018-2019, www.RebeccaMorgan.com

Following are the five elements that mattered most.

 Depend-ability

 Impact

 Meaning

 Psychological safety

 Structure & clarity

© 2019, www.RebeccaMorgan.com

Depend-ability

Team members reliably complete quality work on time (vs shirking responsibilities)

© 2019, www.RebeccaMorgan.com

Impact

The results of one's work; the subjective judgment that your work makes a difference.

© 2019, www.RebeccaMorgan.com

Meaning

Finding a personal sense of purpose in either the work itself or the output.

© 2019, www.RebeccaMorgan.com

Psychological Safety

An individual's perception that a team is safe for risk taking

© 2019, www.RebeccaMorgan.com

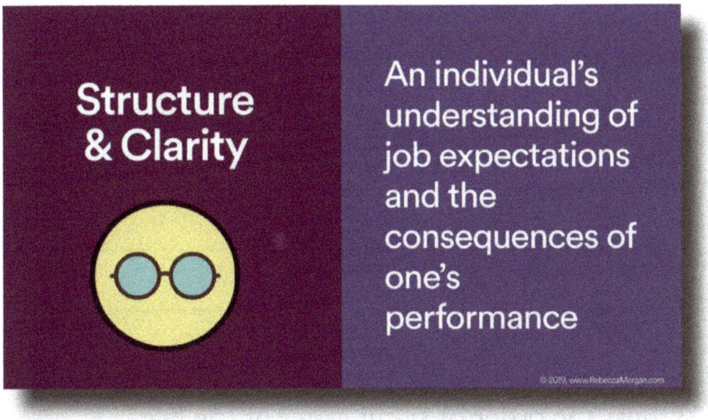

Structure & Clarity

An individual's understanding of job expectations and the consequences of one's performance

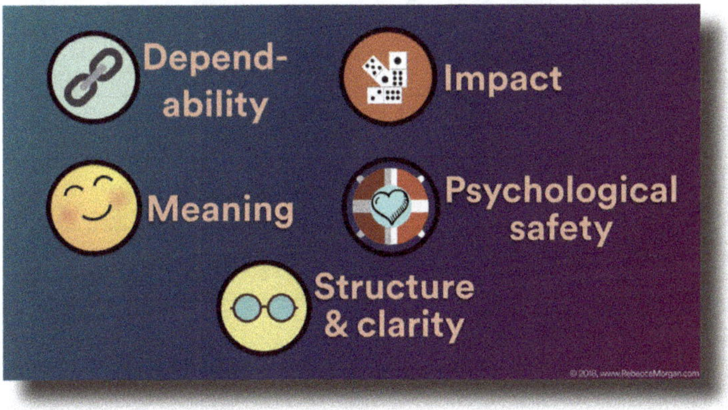

© 2019, www.RebeccaMorgan.com

Depend-ability

Impact

Meaning

Psychological safety

Structure & clarity

© 2019, www.RebeccaMorgan.com

Are you surprised by this list? If so, why?

_____

_____

_____

_____

Are there items among the five that you wouldn't have guessed? If so, which one(s)?

_____

_____

_____

_____

Guess the order of significance of the five.

1. _____

2. _____

3. _____

4. _____

5. _____

Compare your answers to Google's top five.

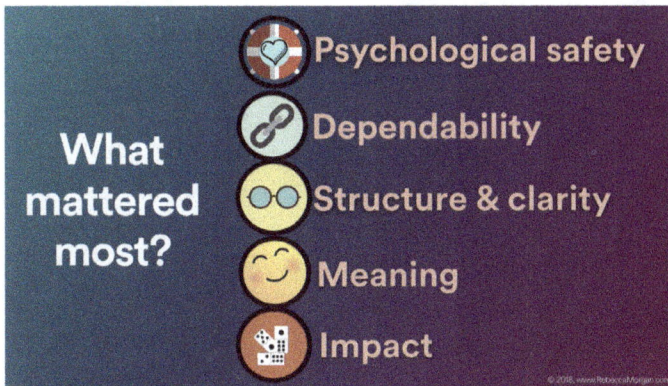

We'll explore each one in depth, starting from the bottom.

I found it difficult remembering all five, so I came up with a mnemonic. The characteristics are not in order of importance, but after "psychological safety," the order does not really matter.

Think of someone with dimples to help you remember DIMPS.

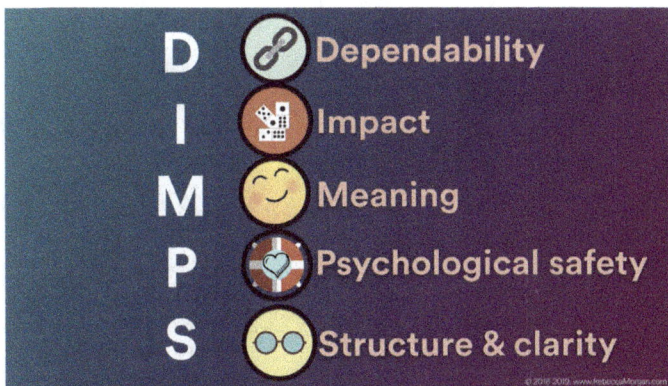

Impact

The results of one's work; the subjective judgment that your work makes a difference.

© 2019, www.RebeccaMorgan.com

When we feel our work has impact, especially when the impact is beyond our company, we have more motivation and satisfaction. We look at the ultimate difference our contribution makes.

Chris Urmson was in charge of Google's self-driving car effort. Now he's started Aurora. I saw him speak at Silicon Valley's Computer History Museum. His quote shows he knows the importance of helping his team know they are working on something big (emphasis mine).

"The most amazing breakthroughs come from teams who like working together, and *people who know they are contributing to something important.*"

Chris Urmson, CEO
AURORA

Glint, a division of LinkedIn, found that of the professionals who had pride in their company, nearly half feel their work has impact on society. This is a tremendous morale and retention tool.

GLINT

Professionals who are proud of the company they work for

46%

have a positive impact on society

© 2019, www.RebeccaMorgan.com

However, it's not always easy to find and communicate that link. Yet it's critical to do so to create a more engaged workforce.

KPMG

Five forces shaping the tech industry CEO agenda

35%

Struggle to link their growth strategy with a societal purpose for their company.

© 2019, www.RebeccaMorgan.com

A useful exercise would be to gather key stakeholders and brainstorm this question.

Steve Jobs understood how critical it is to link one's company with a much bigger outcome. For decades, I've kept an article featuring an interview with Steve Jobs that included this quote:

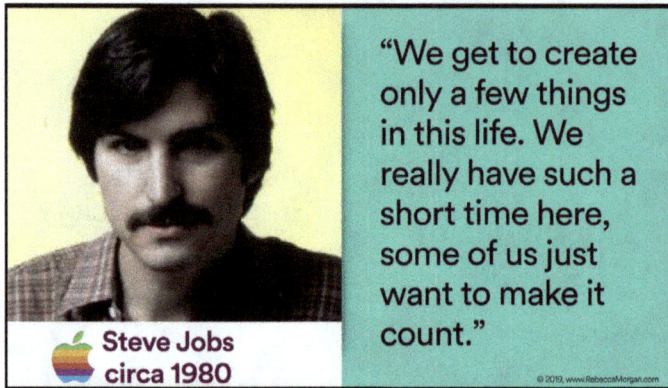

> "We get to create only a few things in this life. We really have such a short time here, some of us just want to make it count."
>
> Steve Jobs circa 1980

Steve was born 2 months before I was and we grew up 15 miles apart. I never met him, although I saw him once at the MacWorld Expo. I couldn't come up with anything more than, "Thank you for the insanely great products you create." How lame! So I didn't approach him. I regret I didn't.

He lived his philosophy every day. He made his brief stay on earth count hugely.

Steve's philosophy carries over to this day, as is exemplified by Caley, who helped me at the Apple Genius Bar. In the course of our conversation about his work, he said something I've never heard from a customer service representative. He knew the importance of his work beyond the immediate transaction.

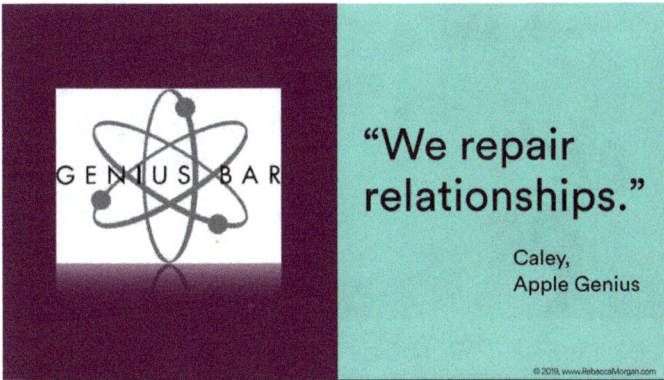

"We repair relationships."

Caley,
Apple Genius

© 2019, www.RebeccaMorgan.com

In his book *Give and Take,* author Adam Grant makes a case for ensuring employees know how their work impacts others.

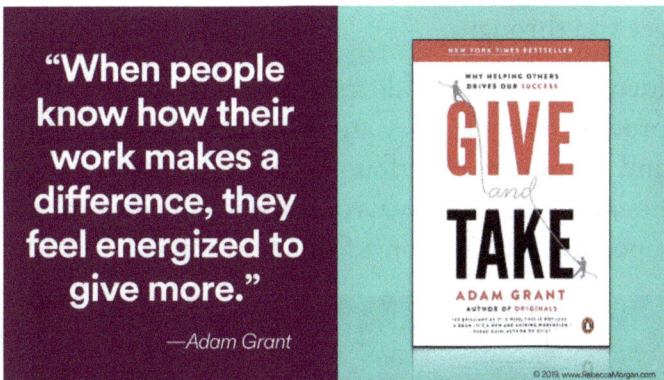

"When people know how their work makes a difference, they feel energized to give more."

—Adam Grant

© 2019, www.RebeccaMorgan.com

When people are energized, they are excited to contribute their best work. They want to do even more.

Recently, I heard YouTube CEO Susan Wojcicki speak at a UC Santa Cruz alumni event. She shared lessons learned in her career. When I heard her say this, I had to write it down:

"Doing something [impactful] gets you through the hard times."

Susan Wojcicki, CEO — YouTube

Photo: TechCrunch © 2019, www.RebeccaMorgan.com

Ms. Wojcicki knows that focusing on the impact of your work helps when not everything goes smoothly. Everyone faces ups and downs. It helps to know you are working on something that makes a difference to get you through.

Ideo designs new products, often reimagining current product designs. They are known for their creativity and innovation. Portfolio Director Joe Brown commented about how focus on impact and purpose have a positive outcome on a firm's bottom line.

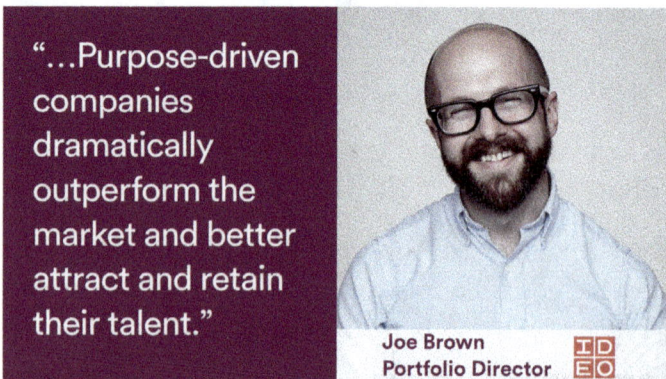

"...Purpose-driven companies dramatically outperform the market and better attract and retain their talent."

Joe Brown
Portfolio Director
IDEO

KPMG sought a way to help their employees understand the impact they made on their customers, and sometimes on society. They launched the Higher Purpose Initiative defined below.

KPMG

"A comprehensive effort to strengthen our people's pride, engagement, and emotional connection to the firm by encouraging them to recognize and celebrate the meaning and positive impact of the work they do."

One of the results is that their employees have a newfound sense of purpose. They are clearer on how their work makes a difference.

Some of the comments reported are simple, but meaningful.

"I fight fraud." "I promote peace." "I protect our energy."

Look at what else KPMG found.

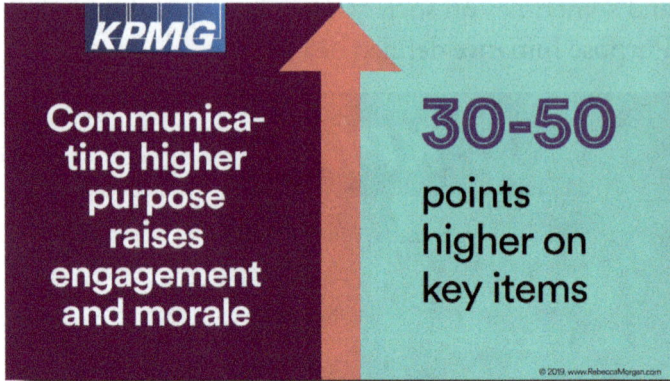

These astonishing findings are from four of the survey questions comparing KPMG's employees whose leaders communicated purpose versus those whose leaders didn't.

Eighty-percent of those whose leaders communicated purpose felt their work made an impact. That's double those whose leaders didn't communicate.

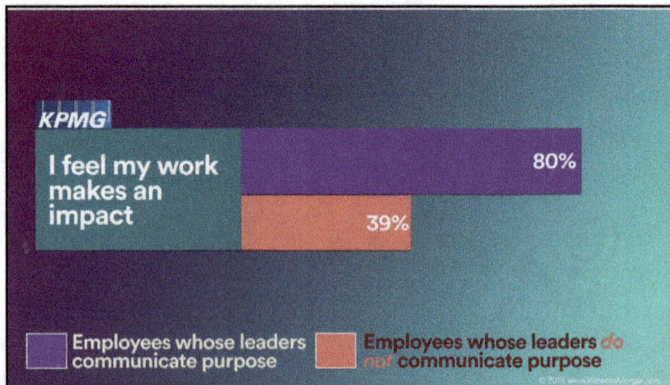

A critical factor of engagement is how motivated employees are to continuously improve. If employees feel undervalued and disengaged, they are not likely to seek improvements. The fact that 91% of survey respondents said they were inspired and motivated to improve is remarkable.

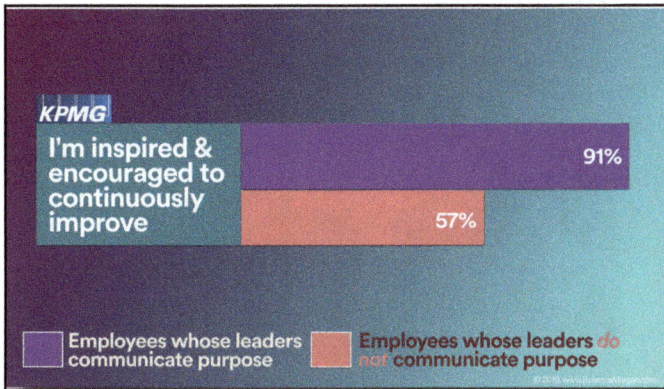

KPMG

I'm inspired & encouraged to continuously improve — 91%

57%

Employees whose leaders communicate purpose

Employees whose leaders do not communicate purpose

If your best people love where they work, they will recruit friends like them. If 94% of your employees say they work at a great place, you will have a steady stream of excellent applicants.

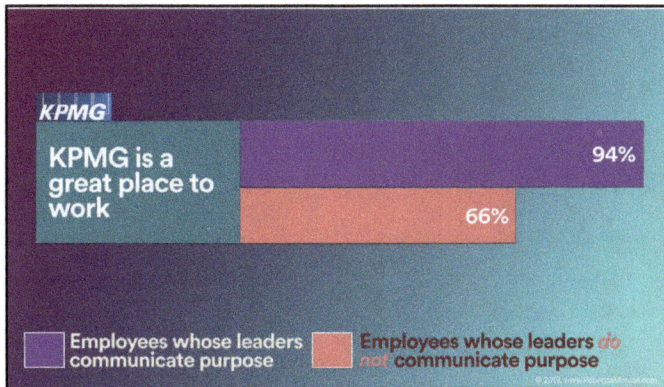

KPMG

KPMG is a great place to work — 94%

66%

Employees whose leaders communicate purpose

Employees whose leaders do not communicate purpose

Having two-thirds of your workforce not interested in looking for a new job outside your company makes executing your initiatives much easier. The costs of recruiting and training new hires are cut dramatically, as you'll have fewer of them.

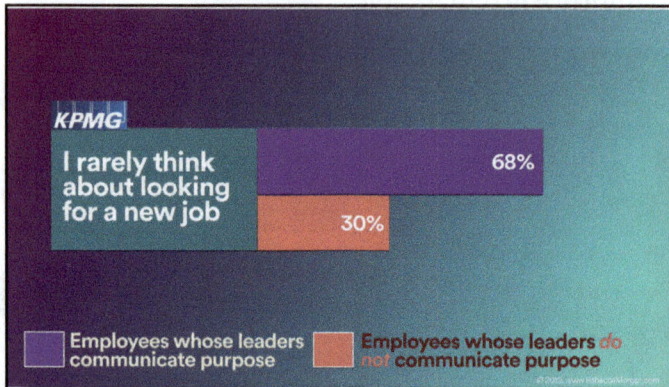

Wells Fargo employees were more motivated when they better understood the real-world impact their low-interest loans were having on their customers. We would think this would be common sense, but the videos helped bring this home for them.

When employees don't interect with the end user, it's harder for them to understand how their products impact their customers. Medtronic ensures their employees hear patients' stories so they know what a difference the products make.

When staff hear patients share how Medtronic's products changed their lives, many employees break down into tears.

from *Give and Take*

© 2019, www.RebeccaMorgan.com

Chris Patton from Fujitsu links helping employees express their creativity with contributing to society. This could include projects that help others in need, outside the scope of one's work. Supporting employees' projects will help them stay.

"Th[e] emphasis on creativity will provoke more employees to look for meaningful work which contributes to society."

Chris Patton
UK & Ireland Head of Marketing
FUJITSU

© 2019, www.RebeccaMorgan.com

Talk to your team about how you all make a difference with your customers, and perhaps society. It will help if you think about this beforehand. Write your thoughts about how your group's work impacts others, within your organization and beyond.

Our work impacts others by...

_____

_____

_____

_____

I can communicate this to our team by...

_____

_____

_____

_____

I will communicate this by (date/time).

_____

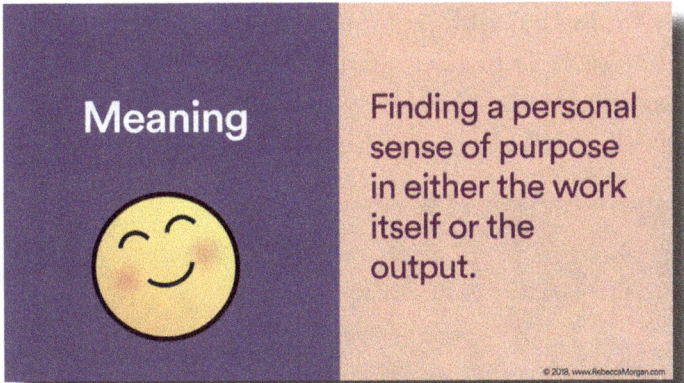

Finding meaning at work is important for most people. If leaders can help their staff feel their work is personally meaningful, the work will be of higher quality, and will create a more effective and pleasant work environment.

Satya Nadella, CEO of Microsoft, understands this and encourages employees to articulate how they find meaning in their work.

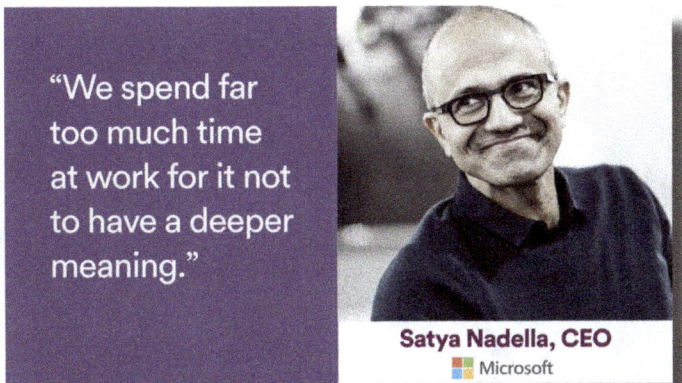

Photo: Brian Smale and Microsoft

Meaning has different definitions for everyone, and may shift as one's priorities change. Here are some common ways people say they've found meaning at work. We'll fill in the fifth one shortly.

The meaning of work is personal:

- Financial security
- Supporting family
- Helping the team succeed
- Self-expression
-

© 2018, www.RebeccaMorgan.com

The first three are self-explanatory. Let's discuss self-expression.

An innovative way Google and other companies encourage self-expression is their "20%" projects. What is it?

20% Projects

Googlers choose to work on a Google-related passion project

© 2018, www.RebeccaMorgan.com

With their manager's permission, a Googler can spend up to 20% of their time on a Google-related project that isn't directly tied to their regular work.

The policy led to products like:

Google News
Instant Autocomplete
Gmail
AdSense (producing roughly 1/4 of Google's revenue)

© 2016, www.RebeccaMorgan.com

Some of these projects have had a significant impact on Google's operations, products, and revenue. All the 20% projects don't result in useful products. As in any experiment, some work out and some don't. Companies which try this are certain to find that the results are worth the risk.

Within their regular job responsibilities, employees may not have the opportunity to work on passion projects. The 20% projects give them that chance. When they do, they are focused, creative, and energized. That motivation can spread to their regular work.

A recent Mayo Clinic study, "Executive Leadership and Physician Well-being: Nine Organizational Strategies to Promote Engagement and Reduce Burnout" showed interesting results:

MAYO CLINIC

Physicians who spend about 20 percent of their time doing work they find most meaningful are at dramatically lower risk for burnout.

© 2019, www.RebeccaMorgan.com

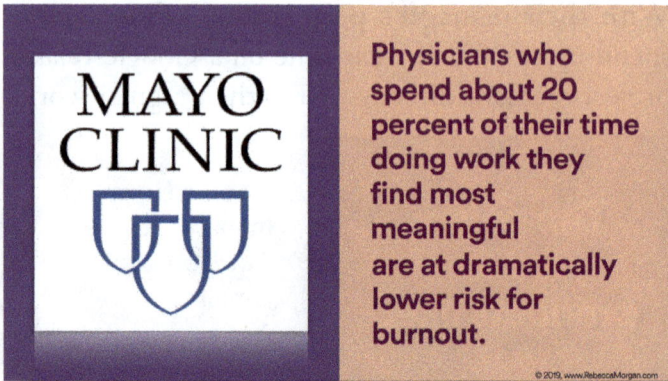

Let's pause for you to reflect on what work you find most meaningful at your job? Start you list here.

_____

_____

_____

_____

_____

What could you do to ensure you do more of this?

_____

_____

_____

_____

_____

Sheryl Sanberg, Facebook COO, expands on being motivated not just by the work, but by the people with whom you work.

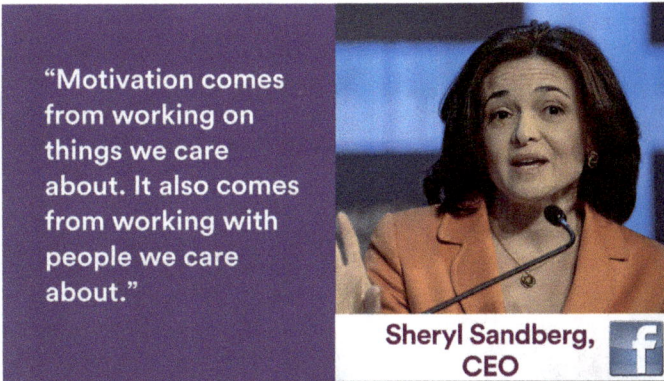

"Motivation comes from working on things we care about. It also comes from working with people we care about."

Sheryl Sandberg, CEO

Photo: World Economic Forum

The last on the list of examples of meaning at work is to grow personally and professionally.

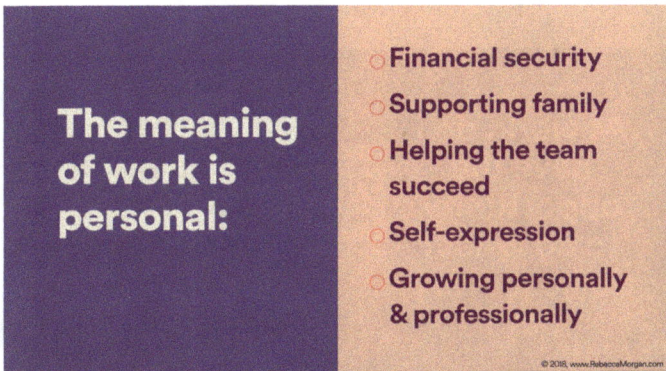

The meaning of work is personal:

- Financial security
- Supporting family
- Helping the team succeed
- Self-expression
- Growing personally & professionally

© 2018, www.RebeccaMorgan.com

The book *First, Break All the Rules* reported on findings of what motivated top-ranked employees to stay in an organization — and what caused them to leave.

Even though the book is not new, the findings are still relevant. The researchers determined their findings by looking at the answers of top-ranked employees versus the rest.

The researchers asked employees 12 questions. Two are relevant to employees finding meaning at work by growing personally and professionally.

These are two of the questions answered "yes" more often by the top-ranked employees than the rest. It is critical that people feel they are growing at work. If they aren't, they are more likely to leave to find an employer who will support developing their skills. If you're not developing your staff's skills, they may leave.

82%

LI employees feel that someone with whom they work closely cares about them as a person.

in
Internal Employee Voice Survey

© 2018, www.RebeccaMorgan.com

This echoes the *First, Break All the Rules* book's findings. If you feel someone cares, you'll want to come to work, do your best and stay. If you feel no one cares, you're likely to do the minimum and eventually leave.

Meg Whitman, former CEO of Hewlett Packard Enterprise and eBay, takes this further, stating the importance to have fun.

"If you have fun at your job, you're going to be more effective."

Meg Whitman
Former CEO
Hewlett Packard Enterprise

© 2018-2019, www.RebeccaMorgan.com

Facebook wanted to see why good employees left the company.

Employees left when they weren't...

- enjoying their jobs
- using their strengths
- growing in their careers

© 2018, www.RebeccaMorgan.com

Facebook, too, found that those not growing in their careers were likely to leave. All three of these items are relevant to employees feeling they received meaning from their work.

You can keep your best team members by applying the following ideas gleaned from Facebook's findings.

Keep good people by...

- providing work each team member enjoys
- helping each team member use his/her strengths
- enabling career development that dovetails with personal priorities

© 2018, www.RebeccaMorgan.com

These concepts are not difficult to understand, but not always easy to apply. When you do, you may have similar results to those found by Facebook. It takes some thought, time and effort.

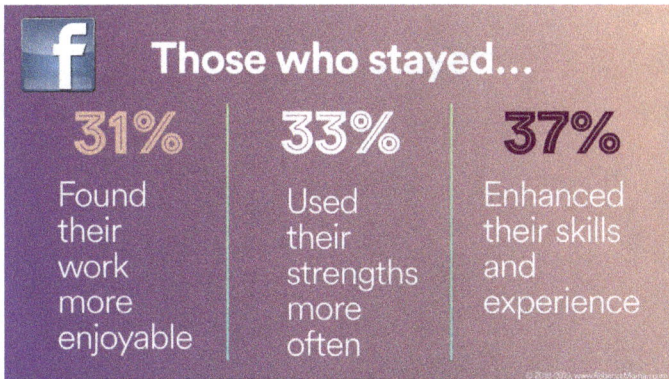

Those who stayed...

31%	33%	37%
Found their work more enjoyable	Used their strengths more often	Enhanced their skills and experience

Facebook employees who stayed with the company showed they felt better about their jobs.

IBM conducted a global survey of 25,000 of their employees. They saw a similar theme where employees want to grow their skills.

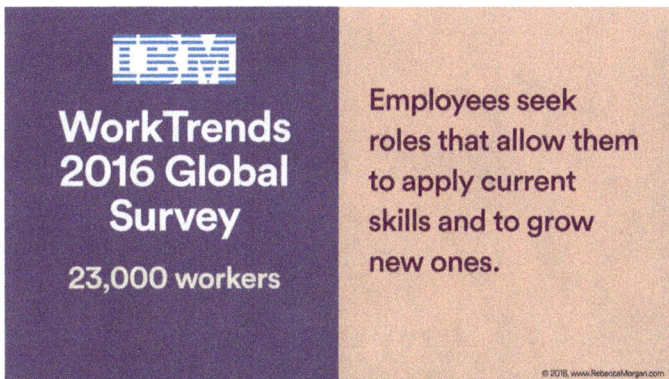

WorkTrends 2016 Global Survey

23,000 workers

Employees seek roles that allow them to apply current skills and to grow new ones.

IBM found professional development is vital to retain the best people and attract others. You may think people are happy at work if they aren't complaining. But they may be seeking other opportunities.

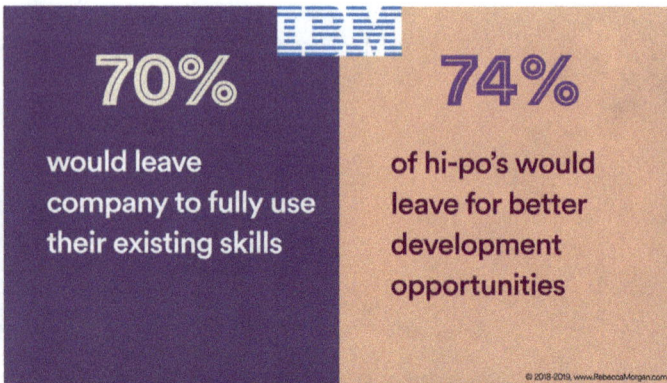

This data shows respondents didn't feel they were fully using their skills. How sad is that?

And the high-potentials — people companies don't want to lose — would leave if they felt they'd receive better professional development elsewhere.

Learning new skills is so important to 65% of respondents that they'd leave their job to acquire them.

The 44% who don't think they have opportunities at their current job may be leaving soon.

Look at what an MIT/Deloitte study found, especially regarding Millennials (those born in 1981-1996).

Millennials, who are in the early stages of their careers, say they get no leadership development at all, even though development is their highest desire.

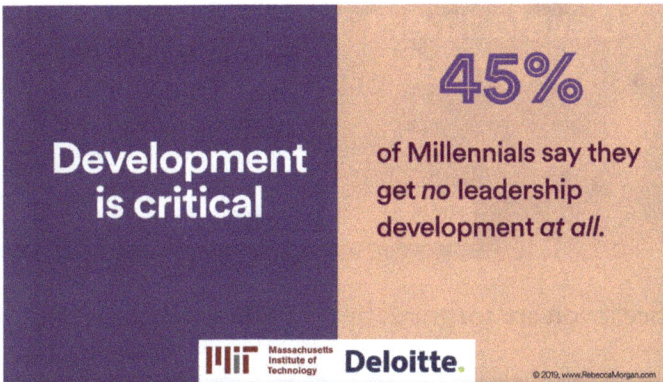

45%

Development is critical

of Millennials say they get *no* leadership development *at all*.

Fifty-five percent of all respondents say their companies aren't giving them enough chances to develop.

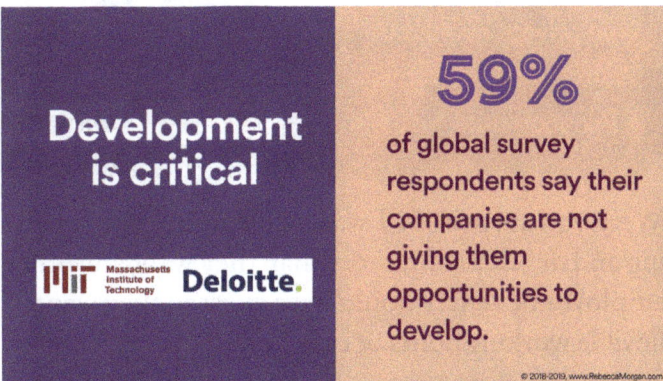

59%

Development is critical

of global survey respondents say their companies are not giving them opportunities to develop.

Across all generations, nearly half of the North American respondents feel their skills will be outdated in three years.

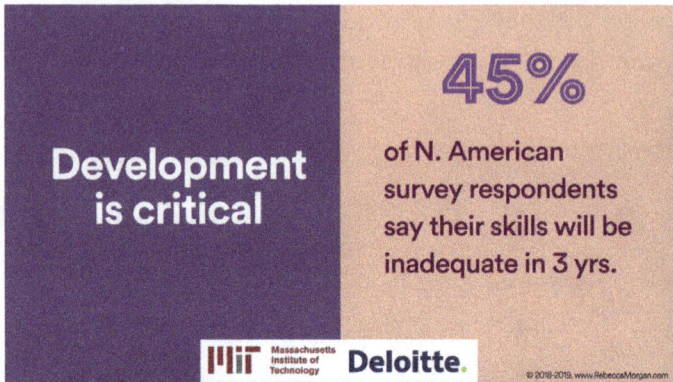

Development is critical

45% of N. American survey respondents say their skills will be inadequate in 3 yrs.

MIT Massachusetts Institute of Technology **Deloitte.**

© 2018-2019, www.RebeccaMorgan.com

See if you are surprised by the Millennials' answers.

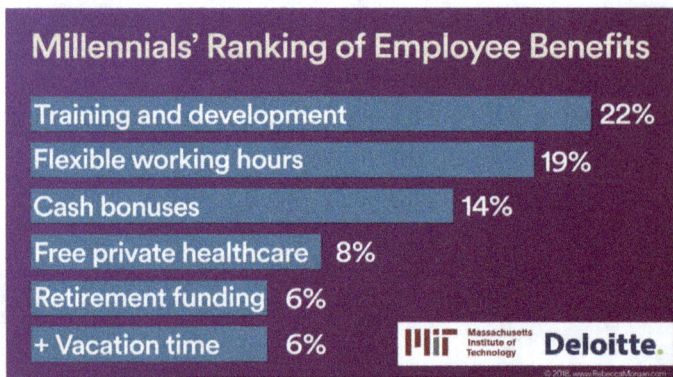

Millennials' Ranking of Employee Benefits

Training and development	22%
Flexible working hours	19%
Cash bonuses	14%
Free private healthcare	8%
Retirement funding	6%
+ Vacation time	6%

MIT Massachusetts Institute of Technology **Deloitte.**

© 2018, www.RebeccaMorgan.com

Were you surprised? I was. Millennials want training and development more than they want any other employee benefit. I would have guessed they wanted flexible working hours or cash bonuses more. Or even more vacation time. But this study said they didn't.

Why don't more leaders invest in developing their people, since the evidence is so overwhelming?

How would you answer? "I don't develop my staff more because..."

_____

_____

_____

_____

_____

_____

_____

A common answer is lack of time. Leaders want their people focused on the job they were hired to do, not taking training courses. The explosion of online learning shows that people think it will improve their skills in a shorter time than attending a class. However, the usage of these skills is minimal. Plus, how can you really ensure some topics, like listening, oral communication, and presentations are really learned without live, face-to-face training? I scratch my head.

As a leader, you can show your conviction in professional development by encouraging your team to continually improve their skills. And since you want to model desired behaviors, you need to continually be sharpening your skills as well, no matter how senior you are in your job. Approach training as a way to refine your effectiveness.

How could you ensure your team members get the development they crave?

_____

_____

_____

_____

_____

_____

_____

Let's look at a way to uncover a new employee's idea of meaning at work by probing some of her interests. Facebook found that when managers asked a new employee about the three items below, it made a tremendous difference. The manager could then strive to give him/her projects she would like.

Start with an *entry* interview Ask about...	○ favorite projects ○ when most energized at work ○ when s/he felt immersed in something ○ passions outside of work

© 2018, www.RebeccaMorgan.com

The *Harvard Business Review* article discussing the findings of the Facebook study included this quote by one of the authors, Wharton professor Adam Grant.

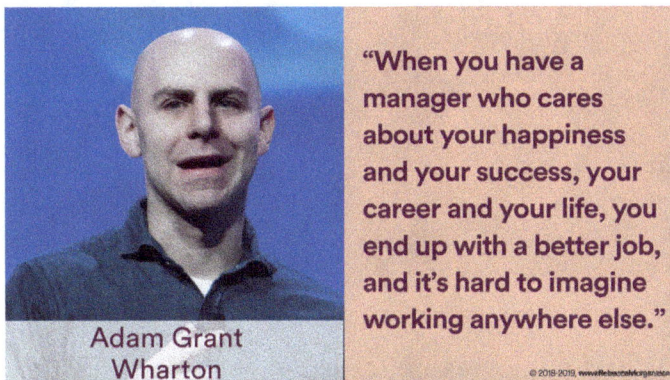

"When you have a manager who cares about your happiness and your success, your career and your life, you end up with a better job, and it's hard to imagine working anywhere else."

Adam Grant
Wharton

Photo: Ståle Grut NRKbeta CC BY-SA2.0

You can see the importance of helping your team members identify and articulate how they derive meaning at work, then making every effort to help them have more of that.

The Harvard Business Review article is at http://bit.ly/PeopleQuit/.

How do *you* connect meaning with work?

_____

_____

How can you discover what your teammates find meaningful at work?

_____

_____

Structure & Clarity

An individual's understanding of job expectations and the consequences of one's performance

When employees aren't clear on job responsibilities, decision authority, or decision process, or expectations, it's easy for their productivity to be diminished. This is common sense. However, it's not common for a leader to see how his own actions contribute to this confusion. To create a highly functioning team, it's important that the basics of your team's jobs are clear.

These include:

Employees must be clear on

○ Job description
○ Decision-making process
○ Rewards
○ Individual & group goals
  ○ specific
  ○ challenging
  ○ attainable

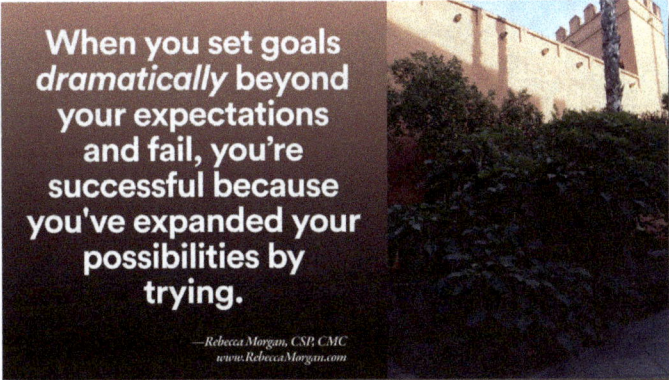

When you set goals *dramatically* beyond your expectations and fail, you're successful because you've expanded your possibilities by trying.

—*Rebecca Morgan, CSP, CMC*
www.RebeccaMorgan.com

Common goal setting advice is to set stretch goals which are achievable but take some effort. Uncommon wisdom is "Don't Focus on Reaching Your Goals.".

How can you ensure your staff have clarity on job requirements?

_____

_____

_____

_____

_____

_____

_____

_____

_____

_____

_____

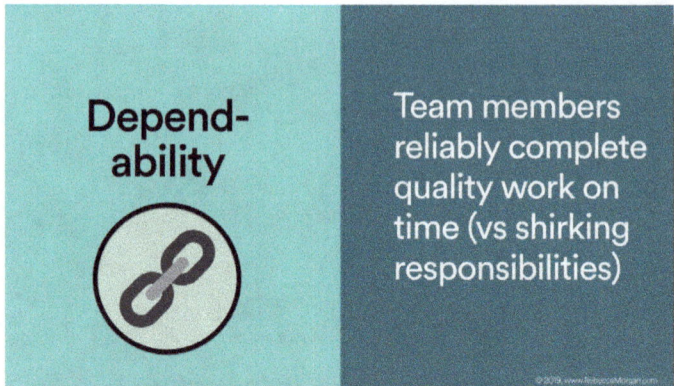

Dependability — Team members reliably complete quality work on time (vs shirking responsibilities)

When team members accomplish tasks well and on time, the whole team runs smoothly. People are energized as they see projects moving forward. The results are positive and the output is of the highest quality.

If dependability is missing, chaos ensues. Blaming is prevalent. Gossip about who's to blame is common. Productivity suffers.

A common psychological test is called "The Big Five Personality Traits Test." It helps people understand themselves better, as well as see that other people may have different ways of looking at the world.

Of the five, we're going to focus on Conscientiousness because it is relevant to our discussion about Dependability.

Take the test to see how you score at http://bit.ly/BigFivePersonalityTest

"Big Five" personality traits	Intellect/imagination (AKA Openness to experience)
	Extroversion
	Agreeableness
	Emotional stability (AKA Neuroticism)
	Conscientiousness

Here are some of the traits exhibited by those scoring high on Conscientiousness.

Conscientiousness Tend to have:	High levels of thoughtfulness
	Good impulse control
	Goal-directed behaviors
	Organizational skills
	Consideration for others

How do those match your own tendencies?

_____

_____

_____

_____

_____

Conscientiousness Tend to:	Spend time preparing Finish important tasks right away Pay attention to details Enjoy having a set schedule Be punctual

How do these match you?

_____

_____

_____

_____

How can you help team members be more conscientious?

_____

_____

_____

_____

_____

_____

_____

_____

(Take the free assessment at http://bit.ly/BigFivePersonalityTest/)

A study at Intel relates to dependability. A pilot program was conducted to see if commonly held uninterrupted time would result in participants' higher productivity.

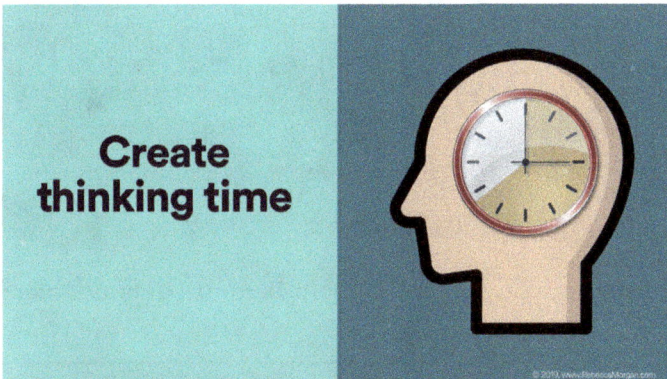

During this "thinking time," participants took measures to limit their interruptions.

4 hours every Tuesday morning **TUE**	○ Set email and IM to "offline" ○ Sent phone calls to voice mail ○ Avoided scheduling meetings ○ Posted "Do Not Disturb" signs at workspace entrances

After the pilot program, participants reported their results.

Results **intel**	○ Enhanced efficiency, effectiveness, and quality of life for numerous employees ○ 71% of participants recommended it be extended to other groups

How can you help your team be more dependable?

_____

_____

_____

_____

_____

_____

Psychological safety is by far the most important of the five elements of Google's successful teams.

Amy Edmonson, Ph.D., a researcher from Harvard, conducted research on psychological safety on teams. She describes the concept:

"…a team climate characterized by interpersonal trust and mutual respect in which people are comfortable being themselves."

Amy Edmondson, Ph.D.
Harvard Business School

Isn't this what we *all* want — to be accepted as ourselves, without judgment? Look at what LinkedIn employees said about being their authentic selves.

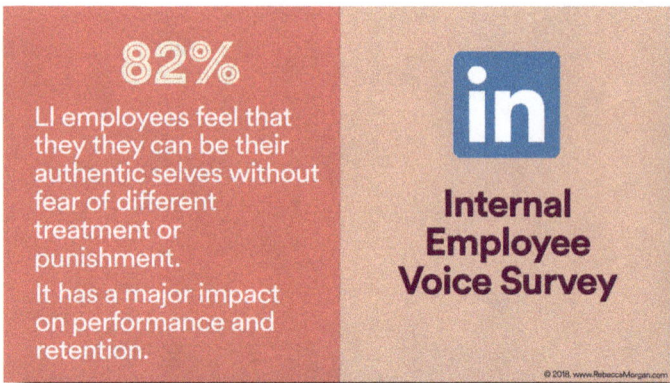

82%

LI employees feel that they they can be their authentic selves without fear of different treatment or punishment.

It has a major impact on performance and retention.

in

Internal Employee Voice Survey

© 2018, www.RebeccaMorgan.com

This freedom to be one's self has a tremendous impact on LinkedIn employees' performance, and retention.

A Glint study showed 47% of respondents who said they are proud of their company agreed it fostered a culture where they can be themselves, ranking it the number 1 reason people stayed at their jobs.

GLINT

Professionals who are proud of the company they work for

47%

Fosters a culture where they can be themselves.

#1

Factor keeping today's professionals at their jobs for more than five years.

© 2018, www.RebeccaMorgan.com

Of course, not all companies cultivate an accepting environment. Some create the opposite — one where employees feel psychological danger.

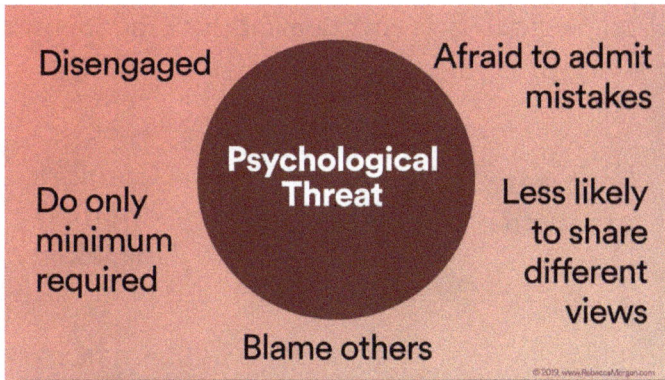

It should be clear that organizations exhibiting psychological danger are much more likely to be toxic, dysfunctional, and have high turnover rates, low morale and low productivity.

My friend Carlos told me this story from when he worked at a Silicon Valley company: "When I shared something vulnerable in a meeting, someone would invariably make a snide comment.

"It was clear one should not admit one's vulnerabilities."

Have you ever experienced a situation (work, school, volunteering, home) where you felt psychologically unsafe? If so, how did it affect your performance?

_____

_____

_____

_____

_____

_____

Psychologically Safe environments have the opposite effect.

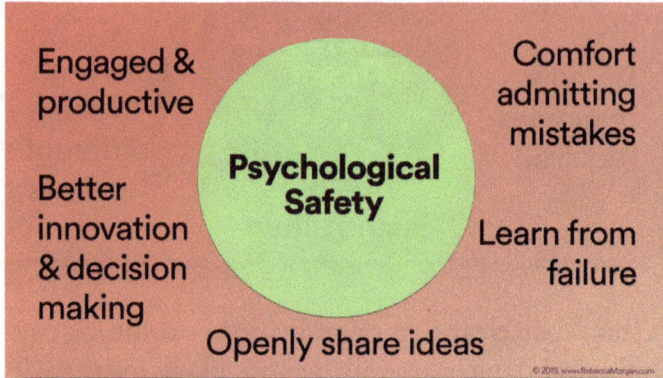

Have you experienced Psychologically Safe environments? If so, how did it affect your performance?

_____

_____

_____

_____

_____

_____

It's easy to see how psychological safety can likely create a highly productive team.

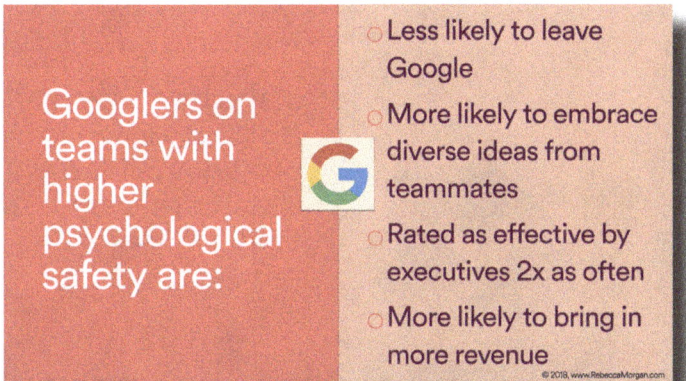

Googlers on teams with higher psychological safety are:

- Less likely to leave Google
- More likely to embrace diverse ideas from teammates
- Rated as effective by executives 2x as often
- More likely to bring in more revenue

© 2018, www.RebeccaMorgan.com

Google's research shows that psychological safety can have tremendous value to a company.

The sales teams' results say it all.

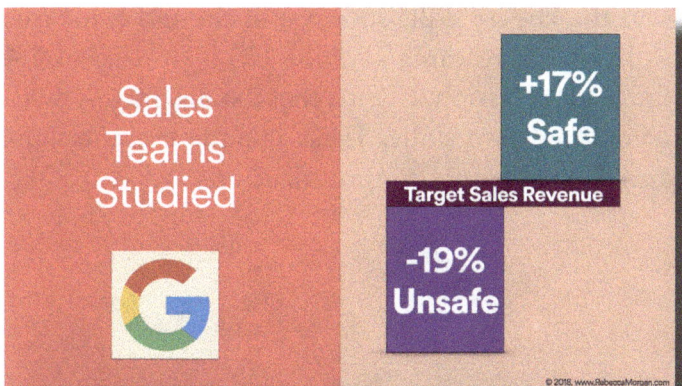

Sales Teams Studied

+17% Safe

Target Sales Revenue

-19% Unsafe

© 2016, www.RebeccaMorgan.com

Wouldn't you love to have your team perform 17% beyond their target? Of course! Let's talk about how to do that.

In the best teams, members listen to one another and show sensitivity to feelings and needs.

© 2018, www.RebeccaMorgan.com

Some may be skeptical that this is just touchy-feely stuff. They may say, "Sensitivity? Who needs that? People need to have thick skins to get ahead in business."

LinkedIn's 2018 "Workplace Culture Trends: The Key to Hiring (and Keeping) Top Talent" report says the largest skills shortage in the US is for soft skills! Their research says the US is in need of 1.4 million professionals with these skills, mostly with communication skills. These include presentations and interpersonal communications.

The largest skills shortage in the US is

soft skills

Short *1.4 million* professionals with soft skills.

Communication is the #1 skill in demand in all 100 metros LI analyzed.

© 2018, www.RebeccaMorgan.com

What were the other two? LinkedIn economist Gary
Berger, Ph.D., shares them:

Top skills shortage:

Oral
communication

Business
management

Leadership

Guy Berger, Ph.D.
Chief Economist

Isn't it interesting that leadership skill is employees'
most sought-after development topic and it's also one
of the top three skills in short supply?

Seth Godin, a well-regarded business expert, makes
a case for the importance of people skills.

"Let's stop calling
them 'soft skills'.

They might be
skills, but
they're not soft."

Seth Godin

Photo: Joi Ito (Seth Godin) [CC BY 2.0

Chris Patton from Fujitsu says essentially the same sentiment.

"As we move into an era of new technological advances, people's value — their soft skills, their communication skills, empathy and sympathy — will greatly increase."

Chris Patton
UK & Ireland Head of Marketing
FUJITSU
© 2018, www.RebeccaMorgan.com

Chris further defines important soft skills in addition to communication. How often have you heard of the need for empathy and sympathy as key elements to leadership success? I've rarely heard these mentioned.

How do you create psychological safety? Let's explore the components and how to implement them. We'll go into depth in each of these.

Creating Psych Safety

Show you're:

- Engaged
- Understanding
- Inclusive in decisions
- Inclusive interpersonally
- Confident and have conviction
- Vulnerable
- Appreciative

© 2019, www.RebeccaMorgan.com

These first six elements are described in the psychological safety research. I added the seventh as I thought it was missing and important.

Let's discuss the first element, Engaged.

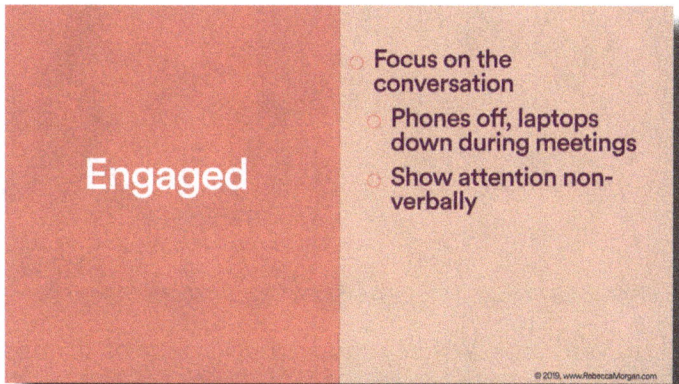

Engaged

- Focus on the conversation
- Phones off, laptops down during meetings
- Show attention non-verbally

© 2019, www.RebeccaMorgan.com

Focusing on the speaker seems like common sense. Yet how many times have you attended a meeting (or even just a conversation with one person) and others are texting or reading email? It's common now.

Some leaders are leading by example by putting their phones in the middle of the table during meetings and asking others to do the same. It is difficult as we've become addicted to our devices.

Many people have forgotten how to show attentiveness to the speaker beyond not looking at their device. Remember to practice the basics: look the speaker in the eye, verbally acknowledge their comments when appropriate, with "uh huh," "I see," "OK."

A concept that dovetails with Engaged is Collective Intelligence. Amy Williams Wooley explains it:

Collective Intelligence

A factor that explains a group's performance on a wide variety of tasks

Anita Williams Woolley, Ph.D.
Carnegie Mellon University

Dr. Williams Wooley studied a variety of groups solving several kinds of puzzles. She found the overall Collective Intelligence was more than five times more important to the team success than the averaged IQ of the team's members.

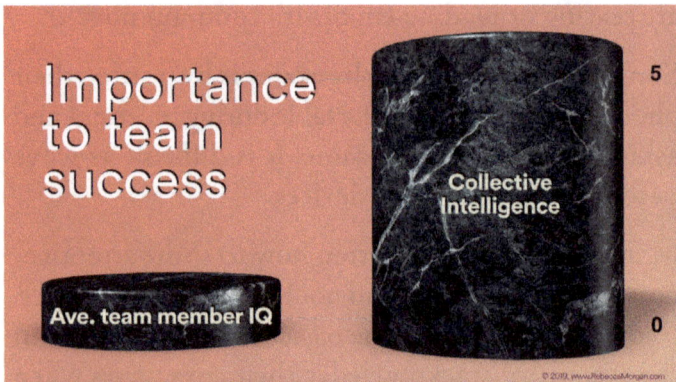

Importance to team success

Collective Intelligence

5

0

Ave. team member IQ

What comprises Collective Intelligence?

How is social perceptiveness measured? Dr. Williams Wooley used a common assessment called "Reading the Mind in the Eyes". You can take it for yourself at http://bit.ly/MindEyes/.

Equality in turn-taking is where no one in the group either hogs the air time or says virtually nothing. Everyone contributes approximately equally.

The presence of a majority of women with at least one man made the most effective teams.

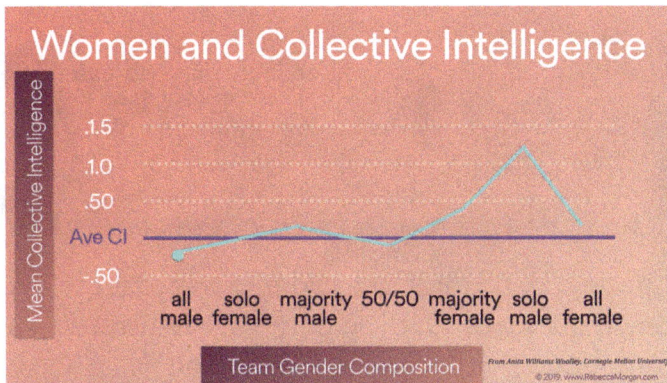

Women generally score higher on social perceptiveness so are better at reading others' signals.

Incrase Collective Intelligence on your team by:

Increase Collective Intelligence

- Set egalitarian norms: everyone contributes approximately equally. No "stars" or loafers.
- Rein in domineering or very negative team members
- Gender diversity

© 2019, www.RebeccaMorgan.com

Let's return to the next item on the Engaged list: Ask questions to learn from colleagues.

Engaged

- Focus on the conversation
- Phones off, laptops down during meetings
- Show attention non-verbally
- Ask questions to learn from colleagues

© 2019, www.RebeccaMorgan.com

Oracle CEO Safra Catz said it is respectful to ask tough questions. But you don't have to use a tough tone. Use a gentle, curious tone instead.

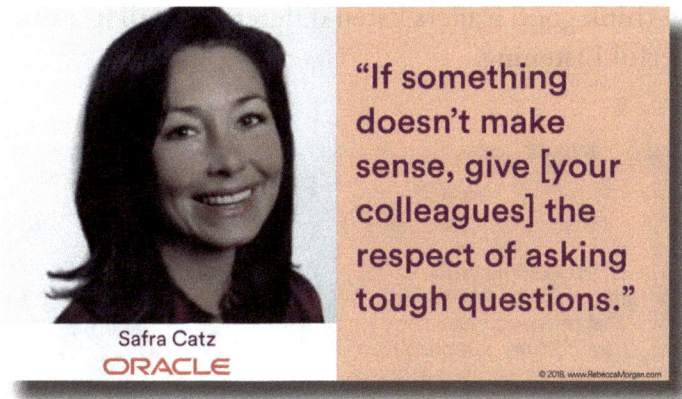

"If something doesn't make sense, give [your colleagues] the respect of asking tough questions."

Safra Catz
ORACLE

The next item on the Engaged list is encourage verbally.

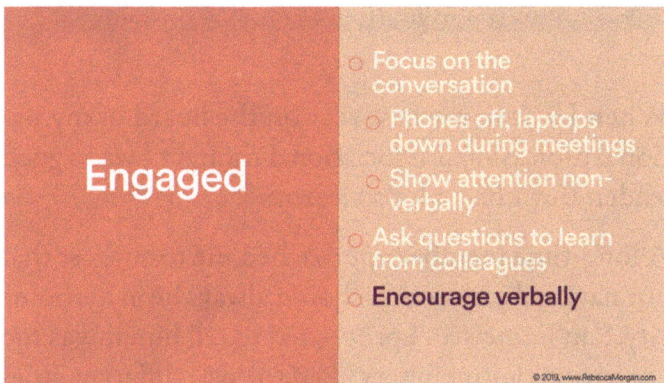

Engaged

○ Focus on the conversation

○ Phones off, laptops down during meetings

○ Show attention non-verbally

○ Ask questions to learn from colleagues

○ **Encourage verbally**

Simple encouragement like, "I like that idea," "Good thought," "That is a good point," go a long way toward people feel good about their contributions.

The last item on the Engaged list is listen attentively. Few people think they need to improve their listening. They think they are already good listeners. Those around them might disagree!

I think good leaders listen differently. I call it "Leaderful Listening."

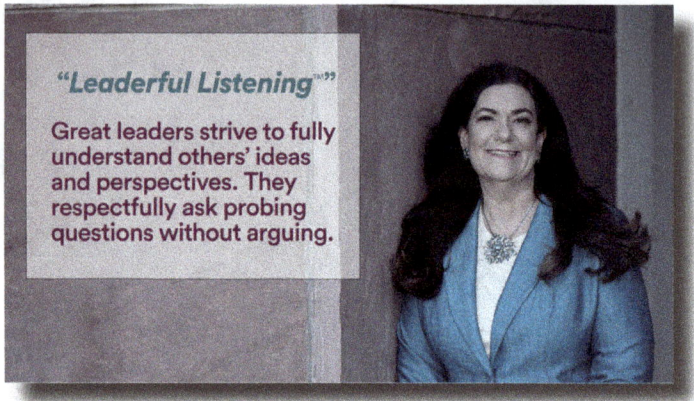

"Leaderful Listening™"

Great leaders strive to fully understand others' ideas and perspectives. They respectfully ask probing questions without arguing.

When I was in my first year on the board of my national professional association, I thought I was a good leader. But I had a lot to learn.

A long-time member approached me to suggest that our national convention should always be in his home city, San Francisco. I proceeded to tell him it was too expensive, our members liked to go to different cities each year, and there weren't a lot of hotels that could accommodate the quantity of meeting rooms we need.

Instead of listening to him and asking him questions, I was essentially saying it was a stupid idea.

Is that how a good leader would listen. No!

Other organizations and thought leaders know how listening well deeply matters.

SurveyMonkey made "Listen to customers" one of their core values.

Tom Peters has touted it's importance for several decades (I added the "or anyone" part).

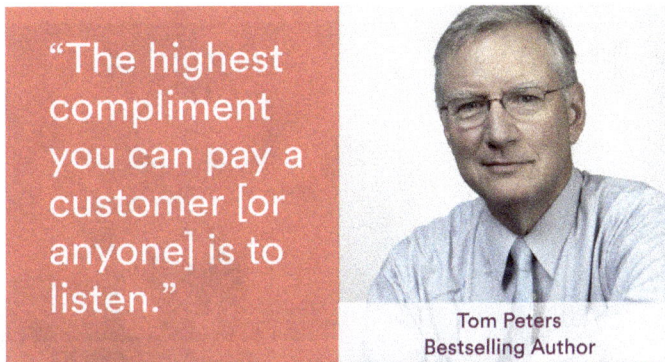

Other leaders have weighed in on the importance of listening. Unfortunately, not all leaders embrace the practice, even if they have said it's important.

After much bad press for Uber, a new CEO embraced a new attitude. Liane said this during the first year of the new CEO's tenure.

"My hope is that we are becoming an employer of choice because of what we have learned and continue to learn by listening..."

Liane Hornsey   **UBER**
Former Chief People Officer

© 2018, www.RebeccaMorgan.com

Carol Bartz shares her feelings about listening to your team.

"If you sit quietly long enough, you find out what people really think."

Carol Bartz
Former CEO   **Y!**

Even politicians understand the importance of this key skill. Winston Churchill's quote is wise — it does take courage to fully listen. You may have to hear opinions that are counter to yours.

"Courage is what it takes to stand up and speak. Courage is also what it takes to sit down and listen."
—Winston Churchill

University of Denver professor James O'Toole explains why some senior managers stop listening well.

James O'Toole
University of Denver

"As one's power grows, one's willingness to listen shrinks, because one thinks they know more than their employees or because seeking feedback will come at a cost."

© 2018, www.RebeccaMorgan.com

How can you better show you are engaged with your team?

_____

_____

_____

_____

_____

It's important to show you are understanding what others are saying. Small gestures go a long way.

Show empathy and compassion

Why is this important? Development Dimensions International recently released their High-Resolution Leadership Report after surveying 15,000 leaders and managers.

They found empathy had the strongest impact on a leader's effectiveness. This is counter to what many have thought about leaders in the past — that they needed to be strong and emotionless.

> **"Overall revenue growth required executives with a broader skill profile, with empathy the interaction skill with the strongest impact on leader effectiveness."**
>
> **DDI**

When someone expresses that she is having a tough time, it goes a long way to respond, "I understand," or "I have been in a similar situation and know it's tough," or "You have my support."

When someone explains their reasoning, instead of arguing or saying how stupid it is, just say:

> 66*That makes sense.* 99

If it doesn't make sense to you, at least confirm that you understood it made sense to him/her with "I can see how that made sense to you." Showing this compassion helps the person not feel stupid, even if their logic isn't clear to you.

The rest of the components of Understanding are:

Confirm mutual understanding

Reiterating your understanding reduces confusion and frustration. Ending an interaction with, "Let me recap my understanding" will eliminate many missteps and rework.

Avoid blaming

Rather than point fingers even when someone else is at fault, you'll gain more fans if you can be gracious, not focusing on the problem but on the solution.

Watch your facial expressions

Do you roll your eyes when someone says something you think is ridiculous? I have. And I've seen the damage it caused. Since your face telegraphs your thoughts and emotions, learn to manage your expressions.

Acknowledge comments verbally

People like to hear evidence that some is listening. Verbalizations of "I see," "Uh huh," and "OK" show the listener you are paying attention.

How can you better exhibit understanding to your team?

_____

_____

_____

_____

_____

_____

_____

_____

_____

_____

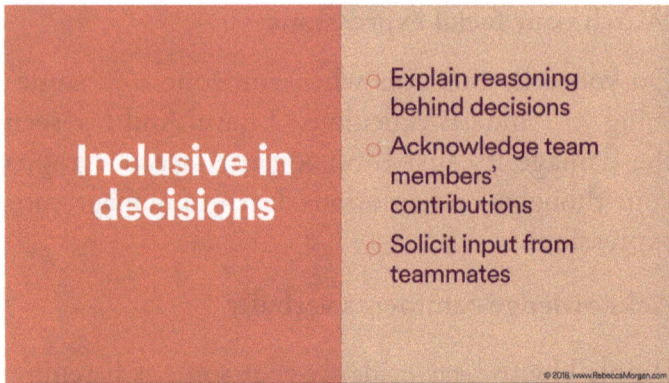

I've not met someone who didn't want to be involved in decisions that affected them.

However, not all business decisions can realistically be made with everyone's input. When you need to make such a decision, at least give your team an explanation of why you made that decision. Understanding your rationale can alleviate some of the frustration of not being involved in the decision.

When the decision is a team effort, make sure to acknowledge the people who helped think through the decision. Honoring people with acknowledgement goes a long way toward showing you appreciate their efforts.

I have been in meetings where my ideas were not acknowledged until 10 minutes later when they came out of someone else's mouth. No one seemed to remember it was my idea and the other person got credit for it! Needless to say, that was frustrating!

If some team members are more reserved in offering their opinion, you can gently ask for their thoughts. They may not have anything new to contribute, but at least they know you want to hear their ideas.

Years ago, a friend shared that this was the most important question in the English language:

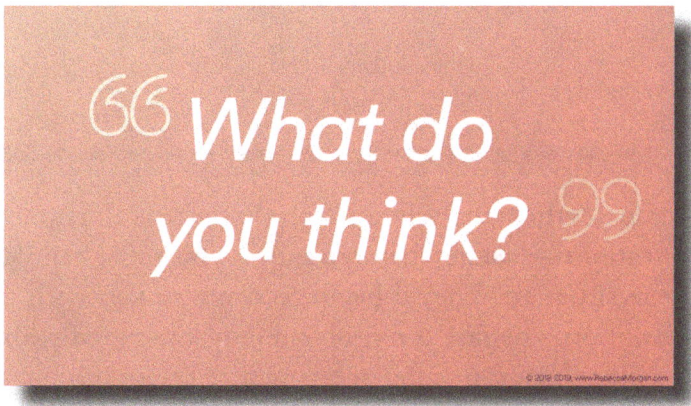

66 *What do you think?* 99

Since then, I've been pleasantly pleased when I've asked people this question. It shows you honor their ideas. It has helped me make better decisions when I hear a different perspective. It can create a deeper dialog as I probe to find out their rationale for their response. It shows that I'm not stuck in my ways and don't think my ideas are always right. And it takes our connection to another level — more of a trusted partner in the arena we're discussing.

If team members ask you for decisions you think they could make on their own, ask:

> ## 66 *What would you do if I wasn't here?* 99

It forces them to think through the options and ramifications — asking themselves how you might handle the situation. They'll begin to come to you with a solution, not just the problem. You can agree with their solution or offer refinements. You're teaching them how to think through problems on their own. Soon they'll just tell you their decision rather than ask you to solve the problem.

> ## Don't shut down others' contributions

When your staff discusses a problem as a group, it's important you and the others don't shut down contributions with comments like, "We tried that before. It didn't work." "We don't need that." "Let's stick to possible solutions, not pie-in-the-sky ideas." Crazy ideas when brainstorming can spawn new ways of looking at the problem, which can create a totally new solution you wouldn't have come up with previously.

Listen to the ideas without shutting down the contributor. I remember being at a brainstorming meeting and every idea I offered was shut down by someone else. I noticed this and then withdrew, not offering any more ideas. I can be creative in problem solving but this group didn't want creativity.

How can you involve your team more in decisions?

_____

_____

_____

_____

_____

_____

Inclusive inter-personally

- Don't allow interrupting or side conversations
- Share personal work preferences
- Ban gossip
- Talk to team members about life outside work
- Conversational turn-taking

© 2018, www.RebeccaMorgan.com

I admit it. I am guilty of making side comments in meetings. However, when the meeting manager makes a point of saying, "Please refrain from side comments or conversations during our meeting." I respect that. So don't be afraid to state the ground rules up front, adding that we all want to be respectful and hear everyone's ideas fully.

When you talk to your staff in your one-on-one meetings, ask how they work best with others. Ask how he likes to receive constructive feedback (I call it "refinements"). Then do your best to treat the person as he has said he wants to be treated.

Gossip is when one shares info about another that the listener does not need to know. It could be personal info about their health, relationship status, or other personal issues. My rule of thumb is each person has the right to share or not share their personal info. Even seemingly positive information is gossip if it didn't come from the source. Nip it in the bud.

Get to know your staff personally, if they want to provide you with more information about their life outside work. Some people are very private and have been burned in the past when personal information has been used against them at work.

If team members want to share about their hobbies and outside activities, welcome them sharing it. If you can support these activities, great. For example, if they are involved in charity work, you can suggest they look into getting a donation from your company's foundation. If they support low-income families through their church by collecting canned goods or clothing, offer to donate to their cause. You know what will work in your organization. Most will appreciate your wanting to know them more deeply.

Conversational turn-taking is important in meetings, but also in one-on-one conversations. Be aware of how much of a balance there is in talking time and ensure you aren't dominating the conversation.

If you notice another staff member cuts off others, or dominates conversations, discuss this in your one-on-ones with him/her. Generally, people aren't aware of this habit and bringing it to their attention can help them curtail it.

Some people think they are connecting with others by teasing them — making fun of a trait, characteristic or comment. Many people take this in stride and laugh along. But more people than you'd think internalize it and feel badly during and after the interaction. Some take it hard and even though they may smile and laugh at the time, it haunts them and affects their self-esteem.

I've vowed to curtail my teasing and humor pointed at others. When joking at someone's expense, I want to be the target of the humor/joke.

Humor, at someone else's expense, can cut more deeply than you'll ever know.

©Rebecca Morgan, CSP, CMC
www.RebeccaMorgan.com

How can you ensure more interpersonal inclusivity with your team?

_____

_____

_____

_____

_____

_____

_____

_____

Confident and have conviction

- Manage team discussions
- Speak clearly and audibly
- Support team to higher ups
- Invite them to challenge you

© 2018, www.RebeccaMorgan.com

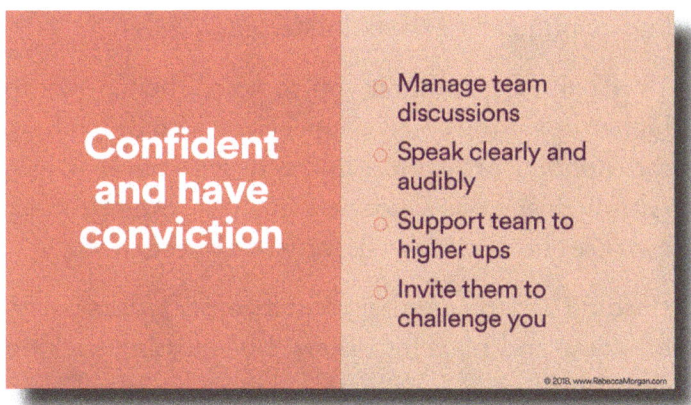

Confidence is one of the most compelling human traits. People are drawn to others who exude confidence. It's part of what we look for in our leaders.

However, when it goes too far, it's perceived as arrogance. Striking the right balance of confidence and humility is the goal.

Confidence and conviction go hand in hand. When you believe in your ideas, you share them with certainty. Others know you believe strongly in them. The trick is to balance conviction with openness to other ideas. Otherwise, you're just close-mindedly stuck in your own, perhaps outdated or uncreative thoughts, expressed adamantly.

Confidence is expressed by the words you say as well as how you voice them. When you speak loud enough for others to hear, rather than mumble meekly, you show your certainty of your thoughts. If people commonly ask you to repeat yourself or speak up, you know you need to speak louder and clearer.

Your team depends on you to voice their needs to higher ups. I once had a supervisor who didn't have the confidence to express my needs with our manager. Although she was a nice person, I lost respect for her because she wouldn't ask for what I needed.

Pushing back on another team member's ideas is easy for some and hard for others. But pushing back on your boss's ideas is difficult for most people. This is why you have to invite your staff to do so, and not slam them when they do.

Pixar director Brad Bird got it right when he first sat down with his team and said:

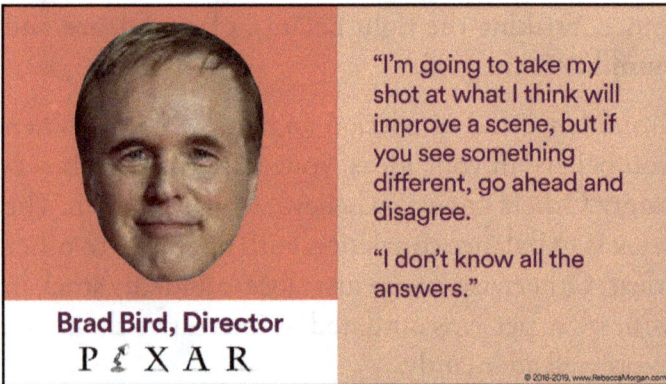

"I'm going to take my shot at what I think will improve a scene, but if you see something different, go ahead and disagree.

"I don't know all the answers."

Brad Bird, Director
P I X A R

© 2016-2019, www.RebeccaMorgan.com

Bird invited his team to challenge him. He knew it made a better outcome. He knew if everyone agreed with him, bad decisions would be implemented. His ego could deal with being wrong.

Netflix's company culture guidelines include several tenets, one of which is Courage. This is one part of it that relates to challenging others' ideas and the status quo.

It can be difficult not to agonize about tough decisions that encourage people to be bold, knowing others will not ridicule you if the decision is made weighing the risks and choosing what you think would be best for all concerned.

This dovetails with the next section on Courage. Being vulnerable can be difficult. We'll discuss this later.

Elon Musk asks others to pick apart his plans. He highly values when others he respects critique his ideas. In a risky business like space travel, automobiles, trucks, and batteries, where invention is critical, he knows many perspectives are needed to achieve success.

"Constantly seek criticism.

"A well thought out critique of what you're doing is as valuable as gold."

Elon Musk

Photo: Steve Jurvetson [CC BY 2.0]

Admitting you don't know all the answers takes strength. Jesper Andersen believes this is critical to success.

Anderson encourages employees to speak out and question the status quo, offering direct and honest feedback to their superiors while also owning up to their own mistakes.

Jesper Andersen
Infoblox

When Dropbox had a dozen people, founder and CEO Drew Houston grew weary of people coming to work at noon. He called a meeting to discuss punctuality — to which he was late!

Afterwards, a staff member came into his office to express how disappointed he was that Houston didn't make a point to be on time to a meeting about being on time! Houston said he's grateful the team member had the courage to speak up, as the conversation was pivotal for him to realize he always had to be a role model.

"He's saying I'm a hypocrite, the rules don't apply to me, I don't respect the team.

"This is what he was hearing or feeling"

Drew Houston, CEO
Dropbox

Photo: Financial Times

"We can write down pretty words about our culture and values. But people pay a thousand times more attention to what you do as a leader."

Drew Houston, CEO
Dropbox

Not all leaders act according to what they say is important. Houston knows that leaders' actions and words carry much more weight than an individual contributor.

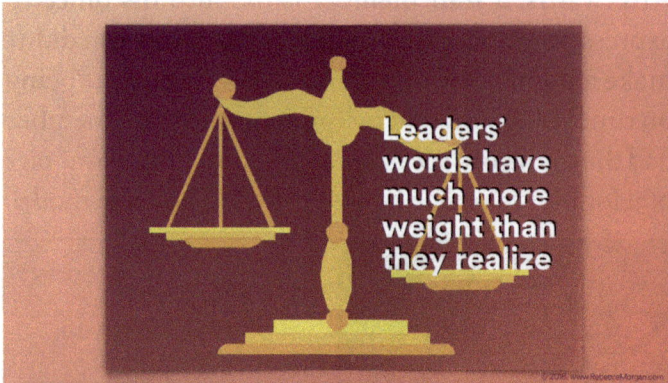

When you are honest with your team members, it's critical that you think through your words carefully. Something you might say to a friend will have much more impact with your team members because you are their boss.

The Honesty Continuum

Since you were a tyke, you've often heard the adage, "Honesty is the best policy."

- ☆ But then your best friend got mad after you told her the boy she had a crush on told you he didn't like her.

- ☆ You lost your first boyfriend after you told him he had bad breath.

- ☆ You ended up in the principal's office after telling your chemistry teacher he didn't explain the experiment well, thus your blowing up the beaker.

- ☆ You were shunned at work when you told your coworker she'd never get promoted since she kept messing up in her job.

- ☆ You got fired because you told your boss his idea of not answering the phones so everyone could get more done would lose customers.

So, is honesty really the best policy?

I believe there is an honesty continuum. On one end of the continuum is complete, unfiltered honesty, as illustrated in the examples above. On the other end of the spectrum is filtered honesty — this isn't lying, but it's not telling the unedited truth.

There are times editing the truth is the best decision for the situation — either the recipient isn't ready/

willing to hear the unvarnished truth, or the risk is too high for you to share completely. You are concerned telling the full truth will cost you your job or an important relationship.

In a perfect world, the raw truth could be told without creating hurt feelings nor negative consequences. But we don't live in that world. We live in a world where people have emotions, egos, and some feel compelled to retaliate against a perceived slight. Honesty — sharing your perspective of truth — can be considered a slight. Some people don't want to hear anything but good about themselves.

How do you decide how much truth to tell and in what way? You have to decide where on the honesty continuum you feel is best for the situation. While people can manipulate the truth for their own gain, it's best to think of both parties' interests. Often thinking, "If it were me, would I want to know? If so, how would I like to hear the truth?" Some people don't want to know. Others want to know but only if the information can be delivered sensitively.

In fact, if you decide to share your truth, I suggest you strive to do so with compassion, thinking through, "How can I deliver my message wih little no pain as possible?" Unfortunately, most people don't give a moment's thought to how their communication might be negatively received, let alone do what they can to mitigate that reaction.

In my three decades working with business people,

I've seen more damage come from not being honest than from being honest. When a staff member isn't performing adequately and the boss doesn't have the guts to tell her so, she is understandably upset when her performance evaluation reflects this. "Why didn't anyone tell me earlier so I could correct my performance?" she thinks or says angrily. No matter when you tell someone less than good news, it will sting. This is why you need to think through how and when you will deliver the message as kindly as possible, and how to be helpful rather than painful for the recipient.

But what if the stakes are too high to tell the whole truth? You can't afford to lose your job or marriage. You withhold some of your truth because you're afraid of the possible repercussions.

I learned this lesson the hard way. While in my fifth year serving on a board of directors, I was one of three board members running for president, elected by fellow board members, not the membership at large.

In the five years I'd served, I became friends with many of the board members. When we got together twice a year, the evening before our meeting began, we went around the dinner table sharing something from our personal lives. Most people shared some family news — generally about kids or grand kids. Since I have neither, I shared some fun personal tidbits, often about my boyfriend-de-jour.

I was running for president for the second time. However, I lost again. I was taken aback, as I'd been on the board longer than the winner, had served in more leadership positions, and had a much longer leadership resume.

Why didn't I win? After some sleuthing, I learned that some board members felt my discussions regarding my dating were unseemly, even though I had been careful to keep my comments G-rated. I thought I was among friends so could let my hair down.

They, however, were observing me as someone who could be the president of the organization. They saw my playfulness and candor as not presidential.

The lesson is, when among those who can help determine your future, don't let your guard down. Be friendly and helpful, but still professional. You never know who is watching — even if they are a peer or subordinate, they could report to and influence those who are making the decision to promote or groom you for bigger things.

Before deciding from where on the Honesty Continuum you will share, be sure you are OK with the possible ramifications from your sharing. You may start out closer to the filtered end and once you see someone is open to hearing more of your perspective, slide a bit toward the unfiltered end.

Please don't interpret the Honesty Continuum as permission to be dishonest and outright lie under the guise of being filtered. There are only rare circumstances where bold-faced lies are acceptable and they usually involve someone's life being in danger.

Use the Honesty Continuum as a tool to help you think through how and how much to share the truth you see. Each circumstance may call for honesty from a different place on the continuum. Think through how your honesty could affect you and others. And work to be compassionate in your delivery.

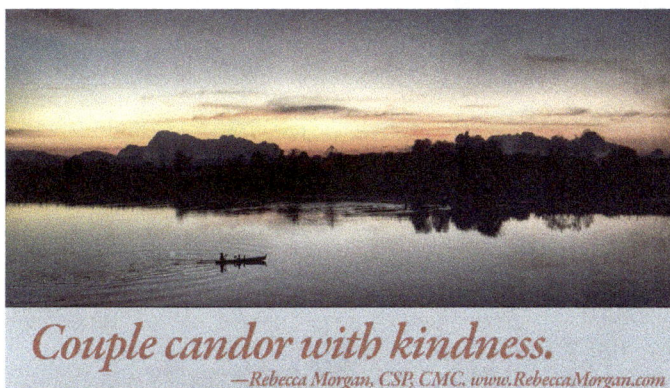

Couple candor with kindness.
—Rebecca Morgan, CSP, CMC, www.RebeccaMorgan.com

Constructive feedback is important to do your best. As a leader, ensure you're speaking kindly as well as candidly.

Until you know you can trust your teammates, it is savvy to decide how honest to be with them. Do you tell them the full truth, or filter it? The Honesty Continuum helps you decide how much to share depending on your desired outcome. You can filter how forthcoming to be or you can be totally unfiltered. Typically, we reserve unfiltered honesty for family and close friends. But some workplaces foster openness.

It is difficult for some people to hear anything but positive feedback. Be sensitive to how someone might hear your honesty. Be kind, choosing your words carefully.

Have you experienced someone who's returned from a personal growth weekend and now is ruthlessly honest? They tell you things about yourself that you really don't want or need to know? In the seminar, they were told to be honest with others. However they weren't told to couple that with kindness.

Honesty, without caring, is abuse.

Rebecca Morgan, CSP, CMC
www.RebeccaMorgan.com

Part of constructively speaking up and pushing back is to push back gently and respectfully.

How can you show more confidence and conviction with your team?

_____

_____

_____

_____

_____

Vulnerable	○ Share life stories, personal struggles.
	○ Share a risk you've taken this week.
	○ Admit failures and lessons learned.
	○ Disclose when you're wrong or don't know

© 2018, www.RebeccaMorgan.com

Vulnerability is hard for many people as they equate it with weakness. When leaders share their current and past life struggles, or what's important to them personally, it can create a stronger bond with his followers. Your staff sees that you are still able and willing to learn, and admit you aren't perfect.

When you regularly take risks, it shows you have courage and aren't satisfied with the status quo. When you share those risks, it encourages your staff to take risks too. Innovation comes from being comfortable trying something new.

Of course, not all new ideas work, especially at first. If you admit to your failures and the lessons learned from them, it inspires others to search for the lessons from their own mistakes. Sharing these lessons with others helps expand others' wisdom.

It's important to say you don't know to your team. It's also important to let them know you can change your mind when presented with more or better information.

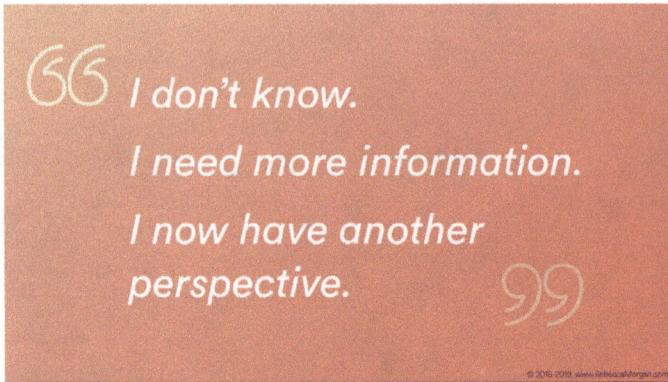

> 66 *I don't know.*
> *I need more information.*
> *I now have another perspective.* 99

When you admit you don't' know everything, have failed, and are still learning, you are showing your vulnerability. But you are coupling it with strength by saying, "I'm working to improve." This creates personal power as people like to follow leaders like that.

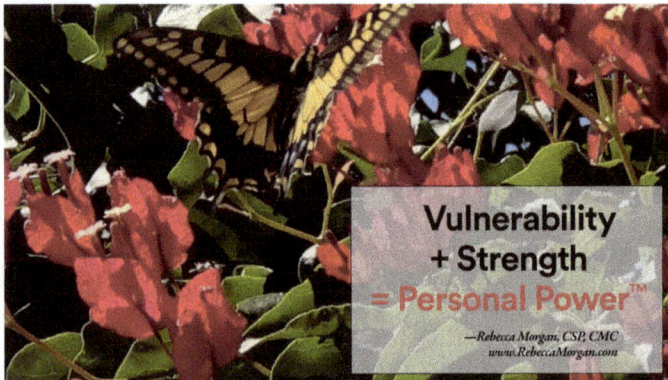

Vulnerability + Strength = Personal Power™
—*Rebecca Morgan, CSP, CMC*
www.RebeccaMorgan.com

Graniterock CEO, Tom Squeri, created a sign to inform his staff of the importance of speaking up when they see someone being unsafe. I liked that he coupled speaking up with courage, and that one needs to accept the message with grace, not defensiveness or anger. This will prevent future accidents and make the work environment safer for everyone.

To accomplish our goal of zero incidents, we need both courage and grace.

Courage to point out an unsafe behavior or condition to a team member.

Grace to willingly accept that feedback when it is offered.

Tom Squeri, CEO
Graniterock

© 2018, www.RebeccaMorgan.com

How can you show and encourage more vulnerability with your team?

_____

_____

_____

_____

_____

_____

_____

_____

_____

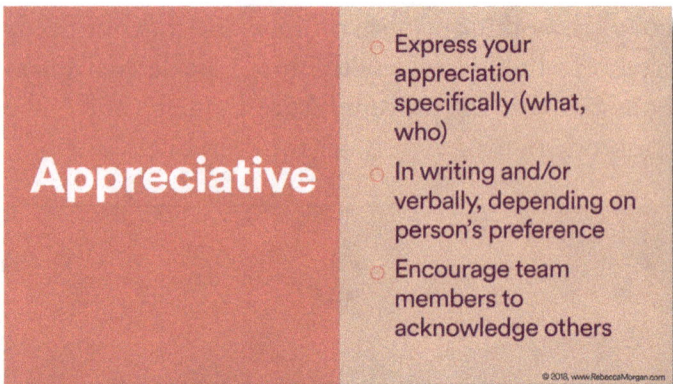

Appreciative

○ Express your appreciation specifically (what, who)

○ In writing and/or verbally, depending on person's preference

○ Encourage team members to acknowledge others

© 2018, www.RebeccaMorgan.com

I've not met anyone who didn't like to receive appreciation. Some may not want it publicly, but everyone seems to like it in some form.

The more specific, the better. "Great job, Fred" does not have the same impact as, "Fred, I really appreciate your extra effort helping Mrs. Gomez with her complicated order. You took extra patience with her. She commented how impressed she was with your service. We both thank you."

Public acknowledgement is embarrassing for some — they prefer to hear praise in private or in written form. Ask each of your team members their preference and then deliver it to them that way.

It's important to think about what you will say to the person ahead of time. Think about how you want them to feel after they hear or read your words.

| How might my comment leave the receiver? | Feeling respected? Or diminished?

Feeling better? Or worse? |

© 2018-2019, www.RebeccaMorgan.com

Clearly, you want the person to feel respected and feeling better about himself. It sounds like common sense, but I've been shocked by the stories I hear of someone's boss "praising" them with ill-chosen words. The receiver feels worse, not better.

Your goal is simple:

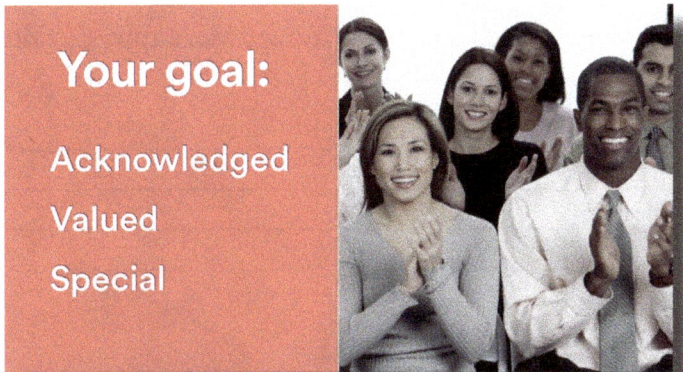

Your goal:

Acknowledged

Valued

Special

When you show appreciation thoughtfully, team members feel more motivated and loyal. People do their best work when they feel appreciated.

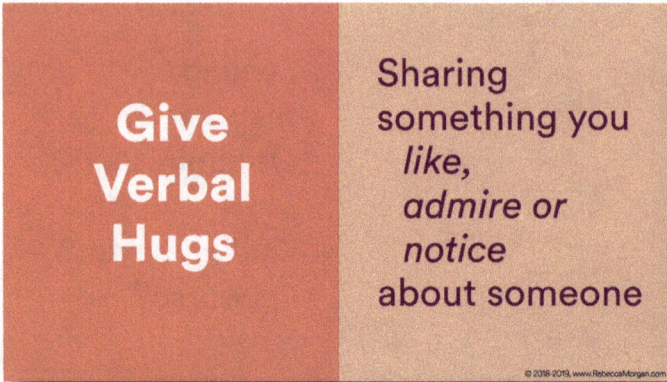

Give Verbal Hugs

Sharing something you *like*, *admire or notice* about someone

© 2018-2019, www.RebeccaMorgan.com

Encourage your whole team to show appreciation for each other. They can do that among themselves. And you can encourage it in group meetings by going around the room and sharing one appreciation for each person. I call this a verbal hug. It needs to be for something the person has done that you admire — avoid anything about their appearance.

How can you show and encourage more appreciation with your team?

_____
_____
_____
_____

Conclusion

The lessons shared are from organizations which are either creating disruption, surviving it, or thriving with it. The studies referenced keep coming back to one key concept — if you create an environment where people feel heard, respected, and acknowledged, they will be loyal, creative, and productive.

You, as a leader, have a huge impact on your team's attitude and performance. How you communicate with them every day sets the tone for the whole team.

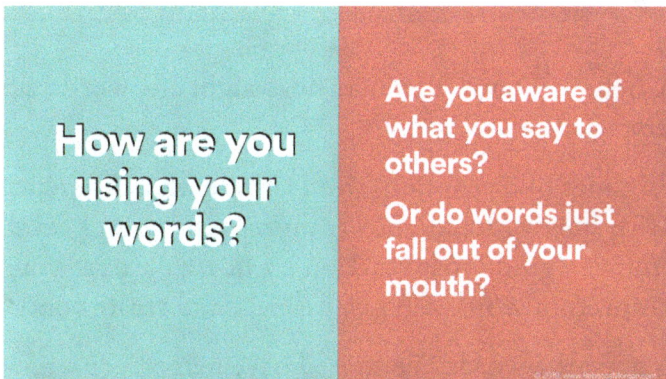

How are you using your words?

Are you aware of what you say to others?

Or do words just fall out of your mouth?

To be conscious of your words takes work. For most of us, words just fall out of our mouth with little forethought. Yet if we give even a little thought before speaking, our words will be much more meaningful. People will respond more positively. There will be fewer misunderstandings.

Our words have more power than we realize. We need to use them mindfully to create the impact we want in our team members, our peers, our bosses, our family, and ourselves.

Words not only affect us temporarily— they change us.

David Riesman, author
The Lonely Crowd

I believe David Riesman was right — words do change us.

In times of disruption, words can make a difference with how you and your team respond to upheaval. You can guide that reaction by how you treat your team. Your words can inspire, heal, and create bonds.

I hope the words I've shared have helped you know how to become an even better leader in these disruptive times. Thank you for allowing me to share my insights.

Rebecca's Related Articles

Disruption

Do You Protest Progress?

Benefits of Intentional Chaos

Are You Resigned to the Status Quo?

Impacct

Apple's Unique Take on Tech Support

Meaning

What's Your Perfect World?

Dependability

Sweating the Small Stuff

How's Your Follow Through?

How Long Will You Tolerate Dysfunctional Behavior?

Psychological Safety

Are You Listening?

Are You Squelching Your Staff's Creativity?

Creating Disengagement

Do You Allow Obtuse, Stubborn Staff to Wreak Havoc?

Give Your Staff Your Opportunity to Shine

Are You a Good Model?

Do You Finesse — or Just Frustrate?

Are You Accusatory?

Do You Protest Progress?

It's no secret that change affects every industry, some more than others. You can protest that change, or you can look at the opportunities within it.

I was involved in a conference for travel executives, including hoteliers, destination management companies, and their clients. One panel addressed cutting edge technologies and how it is beginning to affect the industry. An example was how customers could check in to their hotel via their smart phone on the way to the hotel and get a bar code that would give them entry to their room. There would be no (or much reduced) need for front desk staff.

During Q&A, a young woman protested this technology saying it would eliminate jobs for young people who enter the industry through the front desk. She asked the panelists not to support this technology.

I was surprised by her stance. Many job types have disappeared or been drastically reduced. Today, it is extremely rare to find the following: blacksmiths, typewriter repair shops, eight-track, cassette ,or VHS tape manufacturers. CDs are quickly disappearing. We could go on. Yet I've not heard an outcry from workers in these industries. They learn new skills, move on to other jobs, retire, or make other choices. Protesting progress isn't going to make business people say, "Yes, switching to automated check-in would put front desk staff out of work, so we aren't going to do it."

In the current economic climate it's hard to see the elimination of any kind of job as positive. We need all the jobs companies can provide. But the longer term view is that as technology replaces some jobs, other ones — I'm thinking more interesting ones — will replace them.

Smart people don't complain about the inevitable — they look for opportunities to use their skills and talents in a different way. Or they learn new skills. The key is to be conscious of the budding changes and retool yourself so you're ready.

Who knows what new jobs burgeoning technologies will produce? How can you use your skills and talents in new ways so you're not caught protesting progress?

Benefits of Intentional Chaos

Most people loathe chaos. It causes them a lot of stress. They don't know where to start to create order. They feel overwhelmed and disoriented. Nothing seems familiar.

Why would one create chaos intentionally? Usually it's because we believe life on the other side of the disruption will be better. Often, it is much better.

When you decide to voluntarily move residences, you believe the larger/smaller/differently located lodgings will bring you more happiness. Maybe you've felt cramped in the previous place, or maybe it was too big. Maybe you wanted a better view, safer location, or closer to work or better schools. You were willing to deal with the chaos because you saw the benefit.

I recently experienced some chaos when I decided to turn my home office into a guest room. It was clear the hardwood floor needed refinishing, which meant moving out of the room every item which had accumulated over the last 20 years. After obtaining bids for refinishing the office floor, I learned that it would cost almost as much to refinish the floors in the living room and the dining room. Therefore, I decided to have all of them done at the same. I decided to have them all done at once.

Because of an unexpected hole in the contractor's

schedule, he would give me a very low price — if he could start the next day! I had to move out every stick of furniture and remove everything off the walls in a day. Talk about chaos!

Once I realized everything needed to be removed, I decided to have those rooms painted, as it would be easier if everything was out. Then I saw how dated and dinged up the wallpaper was in the room I intended to convert into a guest room. That had to removed, then the wall textured and painted. While I was at it I added crown molding.

What began as a small job of turning the office into a guest room quickly mushroomed into a major project.

It gave me a chance to reevaluate nearly everything, from the layout of the living room, to adding curtains, getting new rugs, and deciding to change the pictures on the walls. I got rid of anything I hadn't used in years, or didn't represent who I was now. It was refreshing and exhilarating, albeit a lot of work. But as I embraced the new, updated living space, I got energy. The old stuff had weighed me down and I didn't realize it.

The experience also tapped into my creativity. If something didn't work as originally planned, how could I create something that worked?

I noticed I was reluctant to start sorting through the small room where everything got dumped. I also realized that I I didn't know what to do with the accumulation. The task seemed daunting. Where would I begin? I decided to attack it in small chunks.

I'd listen to a podcast while sorting and could stop in an hour when it ended. That made it bearable. I could see the progress after the first hour. In just a few sessions it was back in order.

I saw the value in intentionally creating chaos, whether it's reorganizing your office or your living space. It's probably best for most people to start small with small projects such as a closet or a bureau since too much chaos can feel debilitating. Most of us like some order and completion, so attacking small jobs can create some momentum.

What project could you start on to create some beneficial chaos? How will you mitigate potential stress it could cause you and others? What do you feel the benefit would be once things are in order again?

Are You Resigned to the Status Quo?

There are always circumstances beyond your control. Coworkers drop the ball. Suppliers lose your order. Vendors over-promise and under-deliver.

So you learn to control what you can.

What if you could better manage those whose work you depend on? If you were given an idea to help keep your work on track and on time, would you take it? Or would you shrug it off as "that's just the way it is?"

I'm remodeling my bathroom and love my tile guy. He's fun, thoughtful, careful, creative and a good listener. He's new to having his own business so he's been interested in my suggestions on how to run his business better.

Until today.

He came to finish his work — two weeks past the scheduled completion date. It's not directly his fault, but it is his fault in that he didn't manage his vendors, resulting in their not delivering when he expected.

I started the conversation by asking if there was someone who could do administrative work for him, like making calls to suppliers to ensure their work would be done on time. He said he didn't have anyone as he didn't see the need.

"If you had someone to call the fabricator the week you knew you needed the part, then he wouldn't forget about your order," I explained. "Then we wouldn't be two weeks overdue, so you'd have better cash flow."

"That's just what happens in construction. Things happen and you just work around them."

I wanted to say, "But all delays don't need to happen. You could have prevented all of our delays if you'd been on the phone earlier to check with the supplier."

But I didn't, as I've learned some folks don't have an opening for seeing the world differently than they do. They don't see that a little different process on their part would have a major impact on their customers' satisfaction as well as their own cash flow.

Are there things about which you say, "That's just the way our business is," when really it could be different? Are you resigned because you don't think you could do anything to change it, but you haven't even tried?

Apple's Unique Take on Tech Support

Having some complicated issues with my Mac, I scheduled a Genius Bar appointment.

I took my list of issues to my Genius Bar appointment. I luckily got Caley, a very experienced, patient, and thorough tech who figured out all of my troubles. Some required reinstalling software, which he did graciously. While files were loading, he answered my questions, even recommending third-party solutions and finding them on the Web to ensure I obtained the right product number. One fix helped me save $160 I would have spent on new software.

Since my issues were complicated, it took four hours to get it all straightened out. He politely asked if I minded if he helped others while my computer was installing software. I gladly replied that I did not.

I noticed employees wore three different colored Apple T-shirts. I asked Caley what the T-shirts signified. "These wearing orange T-shirts are the bosses. They help customers quickly get the right help. The folks wearing light blue T-shirts are the sales people. They help people buy the right product for their needs. And those wearing dark blue are the Geniuses. We repair relationships."

Read that again: "We repair relationships." Not "We

repair your equipment." Apple understands that if there's something wrong with your computer, iPod or iPhone, there's a problem with their relationship with you. So a Genius's job is to make sure that the problem is fixed. Thus making people happy with their Apple product. This, of course, creates absolutely loyal fans. Apple is famous for having the highest loyalty percentage in the computer business, with customers, like me, never even considering buying any other brand.

What's Your Perfect World?

My friend, professional speaker and author, Scott Friedman has a mantra for working with others. When exploring a new business relationship, he asks, "What does your perfect world look like for our working together?"

The person then explains what needs to happen — or not happen — to be the perfect situation relating to the job or project.

He says, "I'm going to do everything I can to make your perfect world happen. And here's mine." He then explains what would be the perfect scenario for him.

It's amazing what it creates.

People are enthusiastic about the partnership as they know he's going to work hard to provide their perfect situation. And he's clear on what he would like so they, too, can provide that for him.

If things start to veer from the perfect world, he can say, "This isn't what we described as our perfect world. Do you want to modify the perfect world scenario or shall we reassess what we should be doing?"

Scott has used this when hiring assistants, working with partners and other colleagues. Try it with those you already work with or are exploring working together. See what develops.

Sweating the Small Stuff

I appreciate when people are positive and easy going. However, sometimes one can be too laid back and not take care of details when adopting an "It will all work out" attitude. Then stress ensues, and sometimes even chaos and failure.

Recently I worked on a project with Tom, who had a laid back attitude. I had managed an event for 12 years which Tom was now going to run. I offered to help him manage his event so it would be easier for him to run it the next time. He welcomed the help.

We touched base several times as the event neared, He was open to my suggestions to ensure the event would go smoothly. The week before, I reminded him that we needed five tables and at least a dozen volunteers. He told me both were no problem.

Arriving at the event an hour ahead to help set up, there were five volunteers and three tables. When I asked if more tables were coming he said he'd make some calls and see if he could get more, but if he couldn't, it would all work out.

I knew it would not work with three tables instead of five. I'd tried to run this event with fewer than five tables and chaos ensued. I said, "If we can get two more tables, it will go so much more smoothly." Eventually, the other two tables appeared.

Can someone be too easy going? Yes. When one does not attend to details, it can make things much more stressful than it needs to be. Could we have made do with fewer tables? If we absolutely had to. But it would have made for a much less successful event.

The challenge is how to finesse the message of the importance of details with someone whose philosophy is "Don't sweat the small stuff." There are times when sweating the small stuff is essential. I want a surgeon who sweats the small stuff. I appreciate a car mechanic who sweats the small stuff. I like an editor who sweats the small stuff. I want a product designer who's figured out all the parts and everything works well. I want a pilot who checks the small stuff.

Small stuff does not mean it's unimportant. It's the details, the minutiae, that can make a huge difference between success and failure.

When you're working with someone who equates small stuff with unimportant stuff, it's hard to convince them that the small stuff is worth attending to. They think, "Don't worry." You know that if you don't pay attention to the little things, your project will fall apart. It can be frustrating to work with someone who doesn't have the same focus on detail that will make the project successful. You have to use your best finesse skills to convince them to alter their laissez-faire approach. It's not easy and takes patience.

But the alternative — ignore important details and let the project fail — is unacceptable to you.

How's Your Follow Through?

In my experience, lots of people say yes to things they never provide. Some people even volunteer to do something that never materializes. And they don't even have the professionalism to get back to the person or group to whom they committed to tell them they won't be delivering what was promised.

Two recent occurrences of this reminded me of how rampant this bad habit is.

☆ I ordered some shoes from a store that specializes in shoes for difficult feet. I purposely went in three weeks before a trip abroad and was assured they would arrive before I left. When I hadn't heard anything two days before my trip, I called and was told I would be called back the next day. I reminded the clerk of the time sensitivity and he assured me he'd get back to me before I left. He didn't.

☆ Part of the problem is my expectation that merchants will actually do what they promise. I should know better and take my business to places that have proven their integrity and reliability. However, when expertise is in short supply, we put up with bad behavior. When the competition increases, few customers would put up with this lack of follow through.

☆ When I was remodeling my kitchen, I gathered contractor recommendations from neighbors and friends. Most contractors called me back, but a few didn't. Of those who did, most made and kept appointments to look at the projects. They all promised proposals. About 80% of them sent theirs. When I followed up with the other 20%, they promised a proposal but I didn't receive one. I sent a thank you email to all those who sent a proposal, asking specific clarifying questions. Only about half responded.

☆ Of the final 4, I asked for references. They all said they'd send names and numbers, but only one did. Guess who got the business?

Following through is essential. It shows you're a professional and serious about wanting the business. If you know you can't provide something, don't promise it. If you promise something then find you can't deliver, let the person know. This makes you someone others want to work with, whether on internal projects, or with customers.

It takes diligence to track your promises, and a system to ensure you did what you said you would. But when you do, you'll stand out from those whose promises are empty. You'll show you're a true professional — one that others can count on.

How Long Will You Tolerate Dysfunctional Behavior?

I heard a story recently about an executive displaying highly dysfunctional behavior. She is high enough in the organization to get away with not being disciplined or fired. But she's not emotionally mature enough to understand how her actions have negative ramifications on those around her.

I was told that firing her was not an option. She had some valuable skills and there were other reasons not to fire her. Giving her a written warning was also not seen as a viable option. In the past, talking to her only resulted in her getting defensive and not seeing her behavior was disruptive.

So the organization seemed committed to keeping her. I wondered how long they were willing to tolerate her dysfunctional and disruptive behavior. Because nothing seemed to work to help her change her behavior and they weren't going to fire her. So that only left putting up with the chaos she caused.

All organizations of more than a few people have some dysfunction, some more than others. I'm often hired to help solve these scenarios and even "fix" the biggest perpetrator, as the internal managers either don't have the skills or don't want to deal with the drama. But they are dealing with drama anyway, they just aren't willing to be the ones who try to fix it.

If you aren't willing to create a shift, no matter how messy it becomes, you're doomed to dealing with the ongoing mess the dysfunctional person perpetuates. This may go on for months or even years. Is that what you want?

No. You want the problems this person causes to go away. And that may mean the person goes away. You may have empathy and understand the person has problems in her life which is why she keeps slipping deadlines, not communicating, or having outbursts at work. It's fine to be compassionate and tolerate this for a short time, but it's best to at least call it out when this behavior first surfaces. If functional, professional behavior doesn't ensue, then don't let it slide or it will get worse.

The impact of others having to put up with this behavior is often underestimated. Coworkers have to pick up the slack, causing them stress, overtime, disappointed customers, and/or poor quality work.

My first post-college job was working in a 2-person office with a highly dysfunctional person as the office manager. She called in late or sick at least once a week and often several times. At one point she had no more sick leave left and therefore my boss had to put her on leave without pay. Her home life was a mess. She often hosted late-night parties where drugs and alcohol flowed freely, thus leaving her in no shape to come to work in the morning. Her frequent absences meant I had to do her work as well as my own. Since there were only two of us covering 14 phone lines, when she was out, I didn't get breaks.

Her dysfunction caused the whole department more stress. Finally, she was fired. But the office professionals put up with her behavior for nearly a year before I was hired. I couldn't understand why they were so appreciative that I showed up every day, on time, and uncomplainingly handled both our work loads. As time went on, I saw that my superiors believed office staff showing up on time had been a rarity.

If you are dealing with dysfunction in your work, ask yourself if you're willing to do something about it. If not, how long are you willing to put up with it? If you're not willing to do anything, the answer is forever.

Are You Listening?

John Sculley, former Apple Computer CEO, was asked by a reporter, "If you could change your title from Chief Executive Officer, what would you change it to?"

He replied, "Chief Listener."

Tom Peters says "The highest compliment you can pay a customer is to listen."

Someone once told me, "Most of us are compulsive talkers and selective listeners. Instead we should be compulsive listeners and selective talkers."

We know that listening is important. But if we know it is so important, why don't we listen better?

Often we take others in our lives for granted. We think we know what they're going to say. For example, consider the people you live with — your mate or your children. How do you listen to them?

Now remember when you were first dating that special person in your life. I remember when I first dated my husband. I hung on his every word. He was fascinating. He was so intelligent. He knew so much. He was enthralling. Do you remember such a time? Do you listen the same way now? I work on it every day so I won't take him for granted and tune him out.

Listening well means showing people you're listening. In fact, you can tell when someone is listening. Remember what your parents always said: "Look at me when I'm talking to you." Your body language telegraphs your listening level.

However, some people are good at masking their disinterest. They make eye contact, nod and say "uh huh," even though they're not really listening. Their porch light is on, but nobody's home.

Another reason people don't listen well is because of biases and prejudices. I'm not proud to admit that I've allowed biases to get in the way of my listening well. I became acutely aware of this one day, when my then 15-year-old stepson, Alex, came home with an orange mohawk. When he spoke, I tried to focus on his face, and ignore the distraction of the orange spikes on his head. I brought my attention back to his face, tried to listen, and was distracted again by his skeleton earring.

I realized that I had an opinion about young men who have punk haircuts that live in my house. It didn't bother me that his friends had green, purple, and bright red hair. It didn't even bother me that his girlfriend had a matching haircut! But it bothered me that this young man, living in my house, did. I saw a prejudice that I hadn't seen before.

We all have prejudices. We may not like someone's clothes, make up, speech patterns, or haircut. Yet we need to strive to listen to them fully.

Listening is a critical skill for success. It's not an easy skill to acquire. We can all improve our listening. I hope you see the value in becoming the Chief Listener in your life.

Are You Squelching Your Staff's Creativity?

Business leaders complain that their staff members don't come up with new ideas or creative solutions. Part of the problem can be that there is no incentive to do so. But another reason is staff members are shot down when they do try something new.

This was the case recently during a volunteer experience.

Several times a year I work as a cashier for our library book sale. I like to support our library and community and it takes only 2 hours every 4 months. I also like interacting with our neighbors, as well as snagging some books for myself.

Our group's leaders came up with the idea to make purses by glueing fabric to the fronts and backs of hardcover books and adding handles. They are quite handsome.

But few were selling. Partly because the display was out of the way and there was no price tag so customers didn't know they were for sale.

My team of three cashiers decided to try to increase the sales. We put one especially attractive purse in front of our cash box with a paper on the purse reading "$25."

It was not a perfect solution as every time we opened our cash box, the purse kept sliding down from its perch, dislodging the price tag.

We experimented with putting the display purse elsewhere on our table, but it kept getting in the way. There wasn't a place we could tape the price tag without it harming the purse.

Our supervisor came up to our table and demanded, "Why isn't this purse on the display?" We explained we were trying to increase sales by displaying it on the table since most people didn't notice the rack.

"It just looks sloppy," she said as she snatched it from our table and put it back on the out-of-the-way rack.

Needless to say, we weren't enthusiastic about trying new ways to sell more purses.

How could she have handled it better? What if she said, "That's great you're wanting to increase more purse sales. Let's all brainstorm some ways that we can do that."

But by essentially making us wrong for wanting to be creative, she snatched our enthusiasm when she snatched the purse from our table.

Creating Disengagement

I serve on a volunteer committee that's been meeting every two weeks for 4 months. In my 30 years of volunteering for this organization, this is the most frustrating experience to date.

We have another meeting today. I can't believe how I've gone from fully engaged to now not caring what happens. I'm attending just to fulfill my obligation but I've recently considered resigning.

Here's a recipe for how to turn someone from fully engaged to a hair's breadth away from exiting.

⭐ Make changes to other people's areas of responsibility without their input. They will feel like you're trying to take over; that their work isn't valued, and they will lose any interest in doing anything.

⭐ Ignore input from others. Even if they worked for many hours, don't include their work in what gets moved forward. Or better yet, don't even read it. Offer no explanation on why their work is being ignored.

⭐ Be childish. If someone doesn't agree with you, get defensive. Say things like, "I'm going to put my foot down" or "over my dead body," or "I won't work like this, so I'm not coming to the meeting."

☆ Be terse in your communication. When someone asks for elaboration, give one- or two-word responses. Act like it was a stupid question.

☆ Be stubborn. If someone says they didn't receive something you say you've sent, say you've already sent the info and refuse to send it again. Or imply that they must be an idiot to not have received it.

☆ Insist on doing things your way, even if others don't think that's the best.

☆ "Forget" what's been previously decided and move forward with whatever you wanted, even if the group has decided something different.

I know you're smart enough to know that I'm really suggesting the opposite of the above to ensure anyone working on any project is fully engaged.

Do You Allow Obtuse, Stubborn Staff to Wreak Havoc?

☆ Sally is rigid with customers even though she has the power to flexibly make modifications.

☆ Paul is accusatory to other departments' managers, making erroneous assumptions based on little information.

☆ Bill doesn't carefully read emails, so he asks the same questions again and again, doesn't respond to colleagues' direct questions, and flames them about things that were covered clearly. If Bill takes the time to read the communication, he would spare the staff this sort of discord.

☆ Laurie insists the customer service reps communicate only by text messaging because she claims that it is easy for her. However, it is really easier for them to communicate by email.

☆ Terence stubbornly requires that other managers give him what he wants the way and when he wants it, without any willingness to discuss what would work for both parties.

✫ Sue Ellen gets defensive when anyone suggests a way to accomplish a task that is different from hers, repeatedly citing that any "reasonable person" would see that her way is the only way that makes any sense. She has determined that she is the sole arbiter of reasonableness and is not willing to discuss any other options.

✫ Justin has no concept of "win/win." He only sees "win/lose" and will do nearly anything, at the cost of relationships with customers and coworkers, to ensure he is the one who wins. No one wants to work with him, let alone be around him.

✫ When folks aren't agreeing with her, Theresa makes up what she says the dead founder would have said to do, even though she barely knew him.

✫ Jeremy argues that he is right even though others who are more level headed disagree. He will not back down.

✫ Marilyn cheats on her expense reports and when asked for receipts and explanations, she gets defensive and seems incredulous that she isn't trusted. Only under duress and many requests does she produce partial documentation.

✫ Simon drags his feet on his part of a project.

When cost overruns are certain because of the slipped deadlines, he accuses everyone else of being the problem and says they should be liable for any overage.

Do any of these sound familiar?

These people are wreaking havoc in your organization. They may be costing you customers and/or valuable employees. Their insistence that their way is the only right way is not only off-putting, but also infuriating to those who have to work with them.

They've gotten away with it for so long because they may be the ones with the most knowledge in an area. They've intimidated their boss, they've threatened a grievance or law suit if disciplined, or they are related to someone at the top.

Not only are they dangerous to the health of your department or business, but they can also be literally dangerous if they work in a safety-critical area. I know someone like this who works as an operator in a nuclear power plant, in charge of monitoring if the reactor is running properly. Because this person displays all the behaviors listed above, I wouldn't want to live near the reactor, as this person so frequently misunderstand common communication I wouldn't trust this person to properly interpret communications related to health and safety.

What do you do with someone like this?

☆ Don't put up with the bullying and rigid behavior. Nip it in the bud. Don't let it go or the person will think the behavior is acceptable — meanwhile s/he is alienating your best customers and staff. Don't give into their demands, as that just reinforces that they are "right." S/he doesn't understand that acquiescence isn't agreement. Be professional but firm.

☆ Don't give into their demands, as that just reinforces that they are "right." S/he doesn't understand that acquiescence isn't agreement.

Be professional but firm.

☆ Do what you must to move them on if the behaviors don't change. (Don't plan on them to, as the perpetrator doesn't see anything wrong with how s/he's acting.) You can't afford to have your business poisoned by such individuals. Make sure to do everything by the book as it will come back to haunt you if there were any missed p's and q's.

☆ Give your staff training on how to stand up to overbearing, self-righteous people. Of course, you can't exclude the bully from coming, but s/he will get nothing out of it and may try to belittle and bully the instructor!

Give Your Staff Your Opportunity to Shine

I've worked for bosses who took every chance to be the star of the show, including taking credit for my accomplishments. I've also served under a rare few who stepped aside to give me the spotlight when they could have rightfully taken it for themselves.

Recently I had the latter. While it might seem like a small experience, it meant more to me than I'd have thought.

I was serving on the Global Speakers Federation Leadership Council which oversees 11 international associations of professional speakers. We meet immediately before the US's National Speakers Association annual convention. Part of the opening ceremony is the flag procession where each GSF member country's presidents carry their flag through the audience of 1200 to the main stage. This ceremony is always received positively by the audience with much applause, cheering, and a standing ovation.

The US president, Kristin Arnold, was previously scheduled during the rehearsal, so as one of three other US representatives on the GSF Leadership Council, I was asked to be her stand in for the rehearsal, then brief her afterwards.

Before I found Kristin to brief her, I received a message from Kristin that she'd decided that since she'd be on the main stage numerous times throughout the convention, it would be best to have me carry the flag.

I was pleased, but had no idea how significant the experience would be until I was in it. As the host country, I was last in the procession. Audience members stood up when they saw their own country's flag, or generally stood out of respect. However, when I came down the aisle, anyone left sitting immediately rose to their feet clapping and cheering.

While I'm proud of my country, I'm not prone to flag waving. However, seeing the reaction my colleagues had to seeing their flag gave me goose bumps. I was intensely conscious of pride overwhelming me. I understood that for those brief moments I was representing my 320 million fellow Americans.

By Kristin stepping aside I had an opportunity I'd not had before. I was honored and appreciative of her being clear on how to give her spotlight to someone else.

Are You a Good Model?

I used an assessment in a training I conducted for a client's managers. Everyone really liked the assessment and the insights gleaned from it.

The company owner said he'd like to use the assessment on everyone in his company. "Great" I replied, "I can work up a quantity discount. How many do you need?" He responded, "Don't bother. I got an extra one and I'll just copy it for the rest of the crew."

I was dumbfounded. I hadn't encountered anyone blatantly tell me they were going to rip off the assessment publisher and me. I stammered something about the assessments being copyrighted, but he waived me off with "They'll have to catch me."

Companies are usually savvy about avoiding copyright infringement. But this guy was clueless. He knew the publisher wouldn't do much beyond a cease and desist letter. He was small potatoes.

However, his employees knew he was dishonest and unscrupulous. I'd guess that's the kind of people who kept working for him, as the honest ones would move on. I'd also bet he had a good deal of employee theft as well.

Do You Finesse — or Just Frustrate?

I witnessed a painful (to me) conversation between two male colleagues I admire. I'd been asked by Fred to attend a meeting between the three of us as we serve on a committee together. I asked him the purpose of the meeting and he told me what he wanted to discuss.

During the exchange, I winced as Fred called Sam on the carpet for a promise Sam made to Fred about our project. He recounted a conversation they had 18 months earlier, to which Sam said he had a different memory. It had little to do with the stated purpose of our discussion, so I tried to bring them back to focus.

I've observed both these men finesse difficult conversations adroitly. Yet this time they both succumbed to expressing their dissatisfaction with each other. I was as frustrated as they were with the interaction.

Afterwards, I thought of some ways anyone could finesse a contentious conversation:

- ☆ **Be clear on your communication goal.** When the conversation strays, bring it back to purpose. Don't bring up extraneous topics.

- ☆ **Avoid dredging up past perceived slights.** The other person, most likely, has a different memory or interpretation of events. It only gets him/her defensive, and communication dissolves.

☆ **Don't engage a colleague when you are still feeling the emotion.** Fred admitted to me afterward he was upset with Sam and felt he should let him know. I disagreed, as I thought that sidetracked accomplishing the purpose of the discussion. If you feel you need to air your dispute with someone, do it in a separate conversation.

☆ **Work to not blame or insult the other person.** This should be common sense, but these accomplished, educated men fell victim. It just closes down any useful discussion and gets you labeled as a jerk and shunned from future involvement.

☆ **Be conscious of your tone of voice.** When you raise your voice it sounds like you're yelling, which is neither professional nor effective, and only stirs up the other.

☆ **Work to inquire about steps toward a solution, not lambaste what you think has been stupid decisions.** Ask, "Is there a way to possibly...?" "How could I facilitate your...?" "What do you think the possible solution could be?"

The key to finesse is to be conscious before and during the conversation. If you aren't aware of what you want to accomplish then it's easy to fall prey to emotional triggers that derail the discussion.

Are You Accusatory?

It's easy to get angry and defensive when someone accuses you of something you didn't do.

Yet have you examined if you speak in accusatory language?

For example, a colleague didn't get a recent email I'd sent. When discussing this, he said, "You didn't respond to my email." I knew I had, but was abroad at the time and we both knew I'd had trouble with some email getting through.

I said, "Yes, I did respond."

He said, "No you didn't."

Why would he argue with me, essentially saying I was lying?

I learned long ago to only speak about what you can attest to. He knew he hadn't received the email, not that I hadn't sent it. It would have been less irritating if he'd said what he knew: "I didn't get your email."

But by accusing me of not sending it, his words were inflammatory.

It's a hard lesson to learn, but an important one. When you surmise a colleague's behavior or actions, you create problems. Telling a caller "She's in the bathroom" when really you only know she's not at her desk is making up the truth, even if you know she usually takes her break at this time. Unless you just left the bathroom and saw her there, everything else is conjecture. The truth is "I can see she's not at her desk, but I'm not certain where she is."

Anytime you begin with "You didn't..." see if you can rephrase it to "I didn't receive..." or even "Perhaps I missed it, but I can't find your response." It gives the other person some grace, as they just may have done what you're saying they didn't. Accusing someone is not a rapport builder nor communication beginner. If you want to have a positive, ongoing relationship, don't start with blaming them.

Credits

Photos used with permission.

The logos used in this book are registered in the U.S. and other countries as a trademark of:

Airbnb, Inc.

Apple, Inc.

Aurora, Inc.

Ball State University

Cisco, Inc.

Deloitte, Inc.

Development Dimensions International, Inc.

Dropbox, Inc.

Facebook, Inc.

FastCompany, Inc.

Fujitsu, Inc.

General Electric, Inc.

Glint, Inc.

Google, Inc.

GraniteRock, Inc.

Hewlett Packard Enterprise, Inc.

IBM, Inc.

Ideo, Inc.

InfoBox, Inc.

Intel, Inc.

LinkedIn, Inc.

KPMG International

Massachusetts Institute of Technology

Mayo Clinic

Medtronic, Inc.

Microsoft, Inc.

M-Pesa, Inc.

Netflix, Inc.

Pixar, Inc.

PricewaterhouseCoopers, Inc.

Oracle, Inc.

SurveyMonkey, Inc.

Tesla, Inc.

Uber, Inc.

Wells Fargo, Inc.

Yahoo!, Inc.

YouTube, Inc.

Resources

Go to RebeccaMorgan.com to access a variety of useful resources.

Speaking, Training, Consulting

Engage Rebecca to help your team more effective. Topics are detailed at the website.

Management Articles

Over 500 useful articles designed to help you manage your situations better.

Managers Discussion Guide Program

This program enables you to make your staff meetings come alive in 20-30 minutes per month, with no prep by you!

Books, MP3s and Learning Tools

High-quality tools to help you work more effectively.

Blog

Read new ideas and stories to grow your key talent.

www.ingramcontent.com/pod-product-compliance
Lightning Source LLC
Chambersburg PA
CBHW051737020426
42333CB00014B/1352